ASCENT®
CENTER FOR TECHNICAL KNOWLEDGE

Autodesk® Revit® 2019 Architecture
Conceptual Design and Visualization

Learning Guide

Imperial - 1st Edition

AUTODESK.
Authorized Publisher

ASCENT - Center for Technical Knowledge®
Autodesk® Revit® 2019 Architecture
Conceptual Design and Visualization
Imperial - 1st Edition

Prepared and produced by:

ASCENT Center for Technical Knowledge
630 Peter Jefferson Parkway, Suite 175
Charlottesville, VA 22911

866-527-2368
www.ASCENTed.com

Lead Contributor: Martha Hollowell

ASCENT - Center for Technical Knowledge is a division of Rand Worldwide, Inc., providing custom developed knowledge products and services for leading engineering software applications. ASCENT is focused on specializing in the creation of education programs that incorporate the best of classroom learning and technology-based training offerings.

We welcome any comments you may have regarding this guide, or any of our products. To contact us please email: feedback@ASCENTed.com.

AS-RAR1901-CDV1IM-SG   //   IS-RAR1901-CDV1IM-SG

Contents

Preface

As architects and designers start a project, they frequently think about the overall massing of a building or the area of the footprint. The Autodesk® Revit® software, using its powerful Building Information Modeling (BIM) engine, includes tools for creating mass elements that can be modified into many shapes. You can then apply walls, roofs, and floors to them to continue designing. You can use space planning tools to set up areas for rooms and colors to mark the different areas. For presentations, you can create, embellish, and render perspective views.

The objective of the *Autodesk® Revit® 2019 Architecture: Conceptual Design and Visualization* guide is to enable users who have worked with the Autodesk Revit software to expand their knowledge in the areas of Conceptual Design, including massing studies, space planning, visualization, and rendering.

Topics Covered

* Create In-Place Conceptual Mass elements

* Create building elements from massing studies

* Use Rooms and Areas for space planning and analysis

* Create perspectives, sketches, exploded views, and solar studies

* Render views that include materials, lighting, and enhancements such as people and plants.

Prerequisites

* Access to the 2019 version of the software. The practices and files included with this guide might not be compatible with prior versions.

* You should be comfortable with the fundamentals of the Autodesk Revit software, as taught in the Autodesk Revit Architecture: Fundamentals course. Knowledge of basic techniques is assumed, such as: creating walls, roofs, and other objects; copying and moving objects; creating and working with views; etc.

* Collaboration Tools, BIM Management, and Site and Structural Design are taught in additional guides.

Note on Software Setup

This learning Guide assumes a standard installation of the software using the default preferences during installation. Lectures and practices use the standard software templates and default options for the Content Libraries.

Students and Educators can Access Free Autodesk Software and Resources

Autodesk challenges you to get started with free educational licenses for professional software and creativity apps used by millions of architects, engineers, designers, and hobbyists today. Bring Autodesk software into your classroom, studio, or workshop to learn, teach, and explore real-world design challenges the way professionals do.

Get started today - register at the Autodesk Education Community and download one of the many Autodesk software applications available. Visit www.autodesk.com/joinedu/

Note: Free products are subject to the terms and conditions of the end-user license and services agreement that accompanies the software. The software is for personal use for education purposes and is not intended for classroom or lab use.

Lead Contributor: Martha Hollowell

Martha incorporates her passion for building design and education into all her projects, including the learning guides she creates on Autodesk Revit for Architecture, MEP, and Structure. She started working with AutoCAD in the early 1990's, adding AutoCAD Architecture and Autodesk Revit as they came along.

After receiving a B.Sc. in Architecture from the University of Virginia, she worked in the architectural department of the Colonial Williamsburg Foundation and later in private practice, consulting with firms setting up AutoCAD in their offices.

Martha has over 20 years' experience as a trainer and instructional designer. She is skilled in leading individuals and small groups to understand and build on their potential. Martha is trained in Instructional Design and has achieved the Autodesk Certified Instructor (ACI) and Autodesk Certified Professional designations for Revit Architecture.

Martha Hollowell has been the Lead Contributor for *Autodesk Revit Architecture: Conceptual Design and Visualization* since its initial release in 2008.

In this Guide

The following images highlight some of the features that can be found in this Learning Guide.

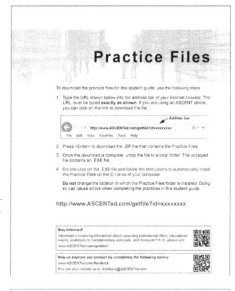

Practice Files

The Practice Files page tells you how to download and install the practice files that are provided with this guide.

FTP link for practice files

Chapters

Each chapter begins with a brief introduction and a list of the chapter's Learning Objectives.

Learning Objectives for the chapter

Instructional Content

Each chapter is split into a series of sections of instructional content on specific topics. These lectures include the descriptions, step-by-step procedures, figures, hints, and information you need to achieve the chapter's Learning Objectives.

Side notes

Side notes are hints or additional information for the current topic.

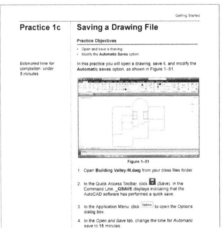

Practice Objectives

Practices

Practices enable you to use the software to perform a hands-on review of a topic.

Some practices require you to use prepared practice files, which can be downloaded from the link found on the Practice Files page.

Chapter Review Questions

Chapter review questions, located at the end of each chapter, enable you to review the key concepts and learning objectives of the chapter.

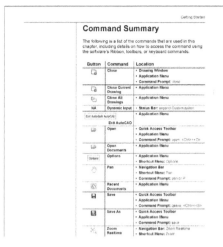

Command Summary

The Command Summary is located at the end of each chapter. It contains a list of the software commands that are used throughout the chapter, and provides information on where the command is found in the software.

Autodesk Certification Exam Appendix

This appendix includes a list of the topics and objectives for the Autodesk Certification exams, and the chapter and section in which the relevant content can be found.

Practice Files

To download the practice files for this learning Guide, use the following steps:

1. Type the URL shown below into the address bar of your Internet browser. The URL must be typed **exactly as shown**. If you are using an ASCENT ebook, you can click on the link to download the file.

Address bar
https://www.ascented.com/getfile?id=yamuna

2. Press <Enter> to download the .ZIP file that contains the Practice Files.

3. Once the download is complete, unzip the file to a local folder. The unzipped file contains an .EXE file.

4. Double-click on the .EXE file and follow the instructions to automatically install the Practice Files on the C:\ drive of your computer.

   Do not change the location in which the Practice Files folder is installed. Doing so can cause errors when completing the practices in this learning guide.

https://www.ascented.com/getfile?id=yamuna

Stay Informed!

Interested in receiving information about upcoming promotional offers, educational events, invitations to complimentary webcasts, and discounts? If so, please visit:

www.ASCENTed.com/updates/

Help us improve our product by completing the following survey:

www.ASCENTed.com/feedback

You can also contact us at: *feedback@ASCENTed.com*

Massing Studies

The Autodesk® Revit® software is a powerful tool for creating accurate building models. When you are just beginning a design, however, you do not need to have that level of accuracy, and may only want to model general features, such as the overall shape of a building. The massing tools help with this initial modeling stage by enabling you to create and modify simple and complex forms directly in a project.

Learning Objectives in this Chapter

- Place and modify massing elements using existing mass families.
- Create mass forms (and void forms) including extrusions, revolves, sweeps, blends, swept blends, and lofts.
- Modify mass faces, edges, or vertices using the 3D Control feature.
- Edit profiles of mass elements.
- Add edges and profiles to mass elements.
- Divide and pattern the faces of masses.
- Create floors at selected levels in the mass.
- Add walls, roofs, curtain systems, and floors to a mass element using the Model by Face tools.

1.1 Overview of Massing Studies

When you start designing a building, you normally do not know its exact size or the locations of doors and windows. You probably do not even know what type of wall system you want to use. In some cases, you need to establish the relationship of the forms of the new building to those of the existing structures around it first, as shown in Figure 1–1. The focus is the overall shape and footprint of the building, which you develop in a massing study.

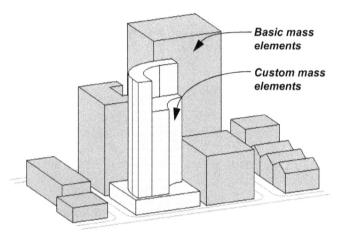

Figure 1–1

- Massing elements are intended for large forms that define the overall shape and size of a building. For smaller elements (e.g., furniture or columns), create or use family elements.

- By default, mass elements do not display in views until the Show Mass mode has been toggled on. In the *Massing & Site* tab>Conceptual Mass panel, select either:

  - (Show Mass by View Settings) - The Mass category must be toggled on in the Visibility/Graphic Override dialog box. Use this if you want to print or export the mass elements.

  - (Show Mass Form and Floors) - Overrides the Visibility/Graphic Overrides and toggles on mass elements and mass floors.

- **Show Mass Surface Types** and **Show Mass Zones and Shades** are connected to the subscription based Mass Analysis tools.

Premade Mass Elements

Premade mass elements (families) can be inserted into a project using the **Place Mass** command. The Autodesk® Revit® software includes several basic massing elements that work like building blocks to help you create the conceptual design, some of which are shown in Figure 1–2.

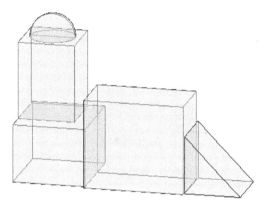

Figure 1–2

Custom Mass Elements

Custom mass elements are created in a project as an **In-Place Mass** or in a separate **Conceptual Mass** family. These families are highly customizable. They are created by drawing profiles, as shown on the left in Figure 1–3 and then applying a form, such as an extrusion (as shown on the right in Figure 1–3) or a loft.

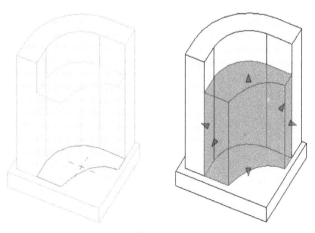

Figure 1–3

Modifying Mass Elements

Premade mass elements can be modified using shape handles in plan, elevation, and section views, as shown in Figure 1–4. Custom mass elements can be modified using shape handles in 3D views and have additional modification options, as shown in Figure 1–5.

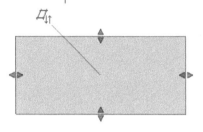

Figure 1–4

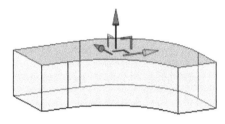

Figure 1–5

Making Buildings from Mass Elements

When you have finished the massing study, you can apply walls, curtain systems, roofs, and floors to the faces of the mass elements, as shown in Figure 1–6, and then proceed to the next step in the design process.

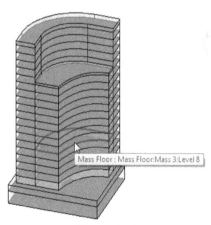

Mass Floor : Mass Floor:Mass 3:Level 8

Figure 1–6

1.2 Placing Mass Elements

The most basic building blocks of massing are the mass families included with the Autodesk Revit software. These include standard building block shapes, as shown in Figure 1–7, which can be resized using shape handles in plan, elevation, and section views, and in Properties for more precise sizing. These mass families need to be loaded into a project.

If you know you are going to use these families in your massing studies, you might want to preload them into a template.

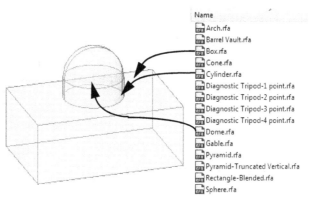

Figure 1–7

- Premade mass families are found in the Autodesk Revit Library in the *Mass* subfolder.

How To: Place Massing Elements

If you have not already toggled on Show Mass mode, an alert box displays stating the program has toggled it on automatically.

1. In the *Massing & Site* tab>Conceptual Mass panel, click (Place Mass). If no mass family is loaded, you are prompted to load a family.
2. In the Type Selector, select a mass type, as shown in Figure 1–8.

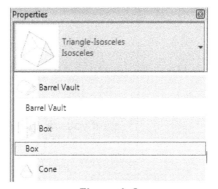

Figure 1–8

*Another element must be in the project for you to be able to use **Place on Face**.*

3. In the *Modify | Place Mass* tab>Placement panel, click either

    (Place on Face) or (Place on Work Plane). Pick a point on the screen to place the mass.

    - To rotate the mass before placing it, press <Spacebar> to rotate it 90 degrees with each press.

    - To rotate the mass after you place it, select **Rotate after placement** in the Options Bar.

Modifying Basic Mass Elements

You can use shape handles to change the sizes of mass elements in plans or elevations (but not in 3D views), as shown in Figure 1–9. This method is not very precise but might be all that you need to do at this early stage of the conceptual design. The shape handle in the center flips the Work Plane.

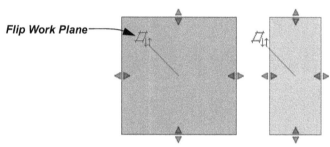

Figure 1–9

- You can make more precise changes in Properties, as shown in Figure 1–10, for a **Box** mass element.

Dimension options vary according to the parameters of the shape.

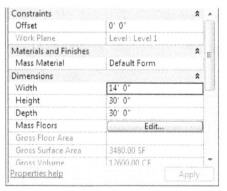

Figure 1–10

- If you want to move an existing mass element to a different work plane, in the *Modify | Mass* tab>Work Plane panel, click

    (Edit Work Plane). Specify the new work plane in the Work Plane dialog box.

Applying Materials

The material (Default Form) for mass elements is transparent by default. Therefore, all of the edges of the mass are displayed, as shown using a Rectangle-Blended form in Figure 1–11.

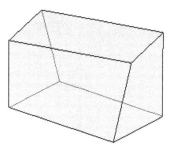

Figure 1–11

- To change the material for the entire mass element, select it and in Properties, change the **Mass Material** parameter to a different material. (This only works for the standard mass elements that are included in the library.)

Practice 1a

Place Mass Elements

Practice Objective

- Add mass elements using existing mass families.

In this practice, you will use basic shapes from the massing families supplied with the Autodesk Revit software to model existing buildings around a proposed site, as shown in Figure 1–12. The footprint and height for each mass are included on the toposurface.

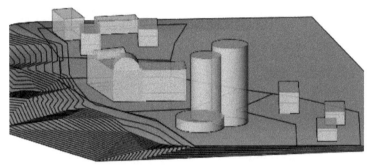

Figure 1–12

Task 1 - Add box mass elements.

1. In the practice files folder, open **Edmon-Towers.rvt**.

2. Open the **Floor Plans: Existing Site** view.

3. In the *Massing & Site* tab>Conceptual Mass panel, expand (Show Mass by View Settings) and click (Show Mass Form and Floors).

4. In the *Massing & Site* tab>Conceptual Mass panel, click (Place Mass). The Box mass element family is already loaded.

5. In the *Modify | Place Mass* tab>Placement panel, verify that (Place on Work Plane) is selected and place several box massing elements on the site plan where you see rectangular outlines, as shown in Figure 1–13.

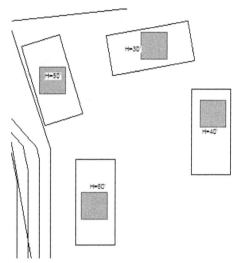

Figure 1–13

6. Select each box and use shape handles to resize them to fit the outline. For the angled sketches, rotate or align the boxes first. When you drag the shape handles, they automatically snap to nearby elements, as shown in Figure 1–14.

7. Use Properties to set the heights as indicated on the existing site plan, as shown in Figure 1–15.

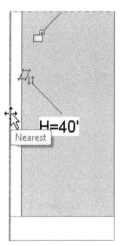

Figure 1–14

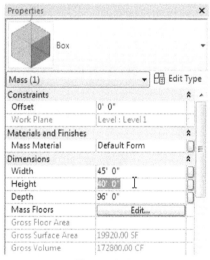

Figure 1–15

8. Repeat the process to add box mass elements to the rectangular sketches in the lower right side of the site.

9. Save the project.

Task 2 - Load and add other mass elements.

1. Click 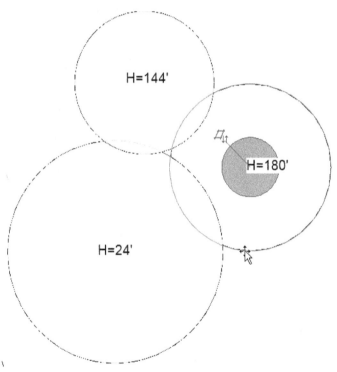 (Place Mass). In the *Place | Mass* tab>Mode panel, click (Load Family).

2. In the Library, navigate to the *Mass* folder and select **Barrel Vault.rfa** and **Cylinder.rfa** and click **Open**.

3. In the Type Selector, select **Cylinder**.

4. Click (Place on Work Plane) and place the Cylinder mass over the three circles. Change the radius and heights to match the plan, as shown in Figure 1–16.

*To position the Cylinder masses at the center of the existing circles, enter **SC** (Snap Center) and select the edge of the circle to place it.*

H=144'

H=180'

H=24'

Figure 1–16

If greater accuracy is required, an In-Place Mass could be created to match the building footprint. For this practice, use two boxes.

5. For the angled building, use two box masses to create the base building, as shown in Figure 1–17. The two masses need to overlap slightly. Set the height of both of them as shown in the plan view.

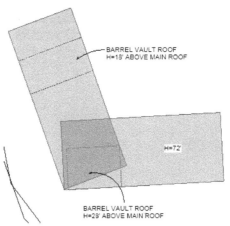

BARREL VAULT ROOF
H=18' ABOVE MAIN ROOF

H=72'

BARREL VAULT ROOF
H=28' ABOVE MAIN ROOF

Figure 1–17

6. Add two barrel vault mass elements using (Place on Face) to place them on the top of the box elements. Align them and then use shape handles to position them, as shown in Figure 1–18.

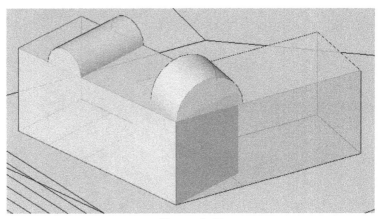

Figure 1–18

7. View the project in 3D.

8. Save the project.

1.3 Creating Conceptual Massing

To create custom massing elements, you need to start with an In-Place Mass where you can create a 3D form from 2D sketches. Masses can be made up of solid and void forms, as shown in Figure 1–19.

If you want to use a massing element more than once in a project, you should create a separate mass family.

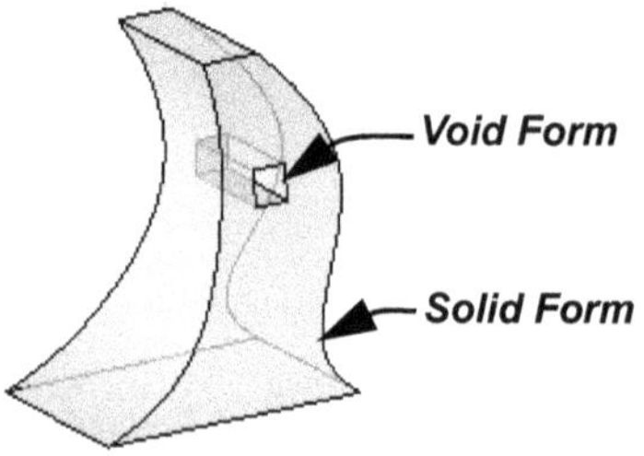

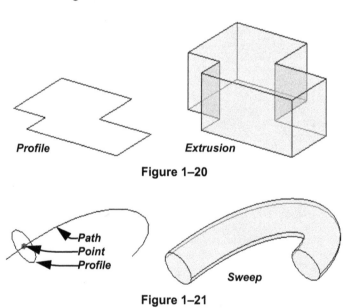

Figure 1–19

Forms are created from a mixture of profiles, paths, and points. For example, one profile becomes an extrusion, as shown in Figure 1–20, while a profile, a point, and path, become a sweep, as shown in Figure 1–21.

Figure 1–20

Figure 1–21

How To: Create an In-Place Mass (Overview)

1. In a project, in the *Massing & Site* tab>Conceptual Mass panel, click ⬚ (In-Place Mass).
2. In the Name dialog box, set a new name for the mass.

3. In the *Create* tab>Draw panel, click ⌇ (Model) and use the draw tools to sketch the profiles, paths, and points that make up the form.

   • Use ⌇ (Reference Line) or ▱ (Reference Plane) as guidelines to help you draw the sketches.

4. Select the profile as well as any related path or points.
   • For the profile, ensure that you select the chain of lines, as shown in Figure 1–22, instead of individual sketch lines, as shown in Figure 1–23

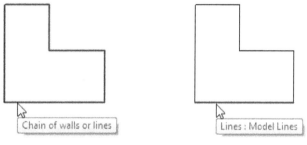

| Figure 1–22 | Figure 1–23 |

5. In the *Modify | Lines* tab>Form panel, expand ⬡ (Create Form) and select ⬡ (Solid Form) or ⬡ (Void Form).
   • A closed profile becomes a solid and an open profile becomes a surface, as shown in Figure 1–24.

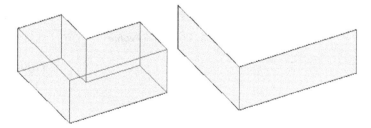

Figure 1–24

6. Click ✓ (Finish Mass).

Types of Forms

Six different types of forms can be created, as shown in Figure 1–25.

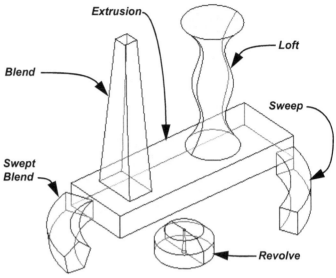

Figure 1–25

Extrusions

An extrusion pushes a single profile in one direction. Although the default extrusion height is preset, you can modify it using the 3D control or temporary dimensions in a 3D view, as shown in Figure 1–26.

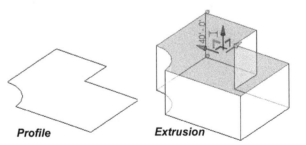

Figure 1–26

- Some profile shapes, such as a circle, have options for the shape of the form. Select the shape from the options displayed on the screen, as shown in Figure 1–27.

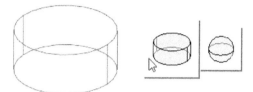

Figure 1–27

Blends

A blend links two profiles together. It is similar to an extrusion but is created when you select two profiles in different planes, as shown in Figure 1–28.

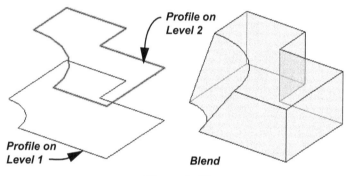

Profile on Level 2

Profile on Level 1

Blend

Figure 1–28

Lofts

A loft connects multiple profiles that do not need to be on parallel planes.It is created when you select more than two profiles in different planes, as shown in Figure 1–29.

Profiles

Loft

Figure 1–29

Revolves

A revolve rotates a profile about an axis. It is created when you select an axis and a profile that are both in the same plane, as shown in Figure 1–30.

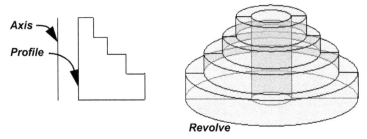

Revolve

Figure 1–30

- When the axis is away from the profile, a hole is generated in the center of the revolve. To create an entirely closed shape, use a reference line for the axis, as shown in Figure 1–31.

- By default, a full circle form is created. To change this, you can select the start edge of the profile, as shown in Figure 1–31, and use the gold arrows to open it, as shown in Figure 1–32.

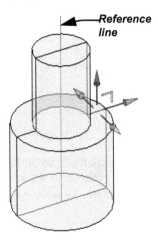

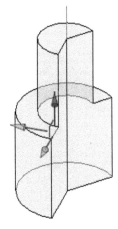

Figure 1–31   Figure 1–32

- You can also modify the *Start Angle* and *End Angle* in Properties, as shown in Figure 1–33.

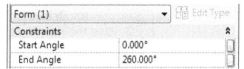

Figure 1–33

Sweeps and Swept Blends

A sweep extends a profile along a path. It is created when you select a path and a profile, as shown in Figure 1–34. The Point Element defines the location of the profile on the path.

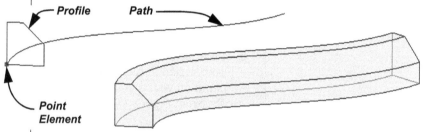

Figure 1–34

A swept blend connects two profiles along a path. It is created when you select a path connecting two profiles in different planes, as shown in Figure 1–35.

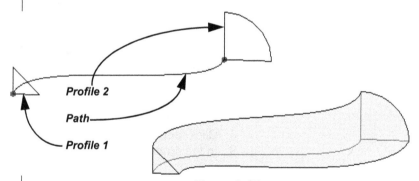

Figure 1–35

How To: Create Sweeps and Swept Blends

1. In the *Modify | Place Lines* tab>Draw panel, click

    (Model).

2. Use the drawing tools to sketch a path for the sweep to follow.

   - A single-segment path can be used with an open or closed profile. A multi-segment path requires a closed profile.
   - A swept blend can only be made from a single-segment path but you can use arcs and splines to create it.

3. In the Draw panel, click ° (Point Element) and click on the path.

   - For a sweep, place a point at one end of the path.
   - For a swept blend, place a point at each end of the path.

4. Open a 3D view if you are not already in one.

5. Click **Modify** and select the Point Element. A reference plane perpendicular to the path is displayed. It becomes the work plane on which you can draw the profile for a sweep, as shown in Figure 1–36.

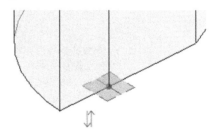

Figure 1–36

6. Use the drawing tools to sketch a profile on the new reference plane.

7. For a swept blend, repeat the process of drawing a profile on the other end of the path.

8. Click **Modify** and select both the path and the profile(s).

9. In the *Modify | Multi-select* or *Lines* tab>Form panel, click

   ⎫ (Create Form).

Void Forms

The process of creating void forms is essentially the same as the one for creating solid forms. The only difference is that void forms are designed to be inside a solid form so that it has a solid element to cut out, as shown in Figure 1–37.

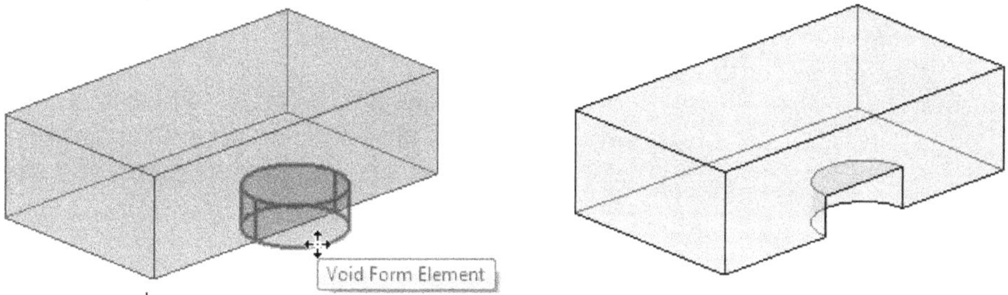

Figure 1–37

You can change a form from solid to void. Select the solid form and in Properties in the *Identity Data* area, change the *Solid/Void* parameter, as shown in Figure 1–38.

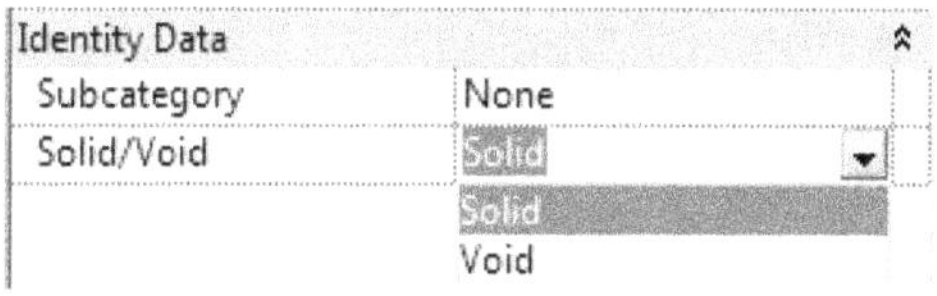

Figure 1–38

Hint: Cutting Solid Forms with Other Solid Forms

If you have two solid forms that overlap, you can use (Cut Geometry) to cut out one of the forms, as shown in Figure 1–39.

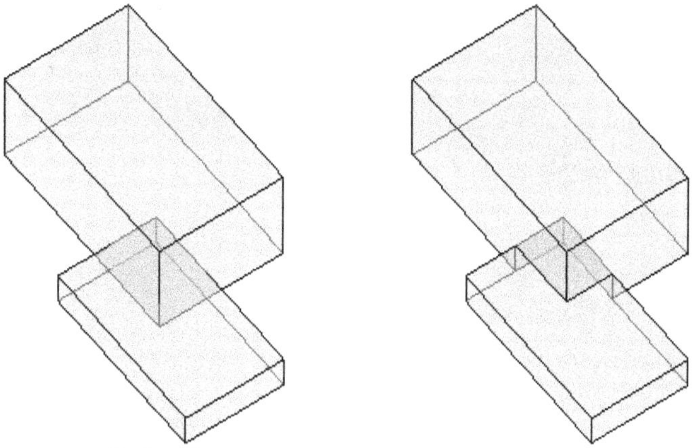

Before Cut ***After Cut***

Figure 1–39

- The first form selected is cut and the second form selected remains as is.

1.4 Setting the Work Plane

Profiles and paths are the building blocks of the mass form elements. They are sketched on the current work plane which can be a face, as shown in Figure 1–40, or a specified work plane, as shown in Figure 1–41.

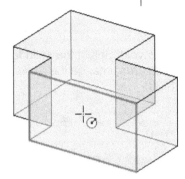

Figure 1–40

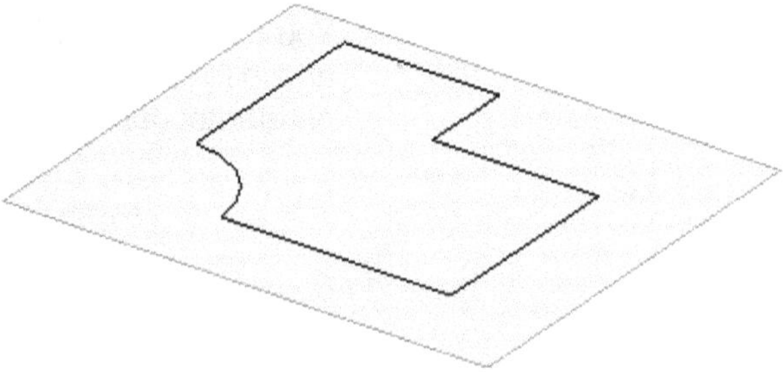

Figure 1–41

- If you are in a plan view, the related level is the active work plane by default.

How To: Establish a Work Plane by Face

1. In the *Create* tab>Draw panel, select a sketching tool.

2. In the *Modify | Place Lines* tab>Draw panel, click 🖌 (Draw on Face). This is typically selected by default.

3. Hover the cursor over the face of an existing element. It highlights and you can then draw the sketch, as shown in Figure 1–42.

Sketches can be locked to faces.

Press <Tab> to cycle through nearby faces.

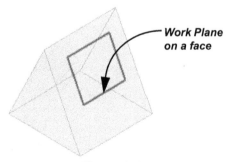

Work Plane on a face

Figure 1–42

4. You can move directly to another face and continue drawing sketches.

How To: Establish a Work Plane by Placement Plane

1. In the *Create* tab>Draw panel, select a sketching tool. The active work plane displays with a heavy outline.

To display the work plane in a view, in the Work Plane panel, click

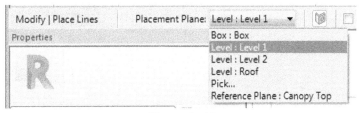 *(Show),*

2. In the *Modify | Place Lines* tab>Draw panel, click 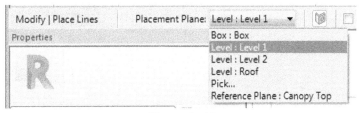 (Draw on Work Plane).

3. In the Options Bar, in the *Placement Plane* drop-down list, select a *Level* or named Reference Plane, as shown in Figure 1–43.

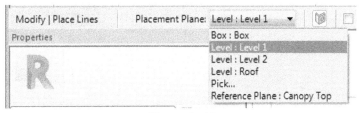

Figure 1–43

- This list varies according to the elements contained in the massing study.

4. Draw the sketch on the plane, as shown in Figure 1–44.

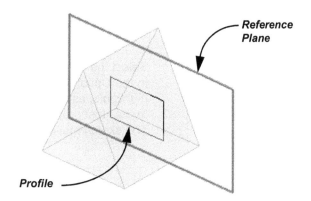

Figure 1–44

- If you have used the **Pick...** option, the selected face becomes the active work plane.

Hint: Naming Reference Planes

You can name reference planes so that they can be specified as a work plane. Select the reference plane and *<Click to name>* or in Properties, set a *Name*, as shown in Figure 1–45.

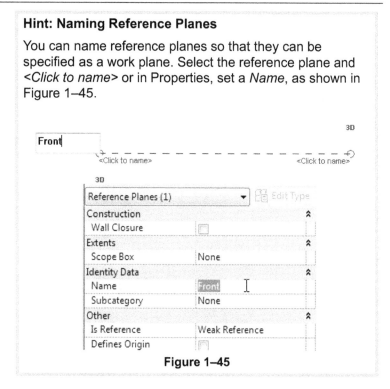

Figure 1–45

How To: Change the Work Plane of a Sketch or Form

1. Select the sketch or form.
2. In the Options Bar, click **Show Host**. The host work plane highlights, as shown in Figure 1–46.
3. In the Host drop-down list, select a new host for the sketch. The sketch moves to the selected plane.

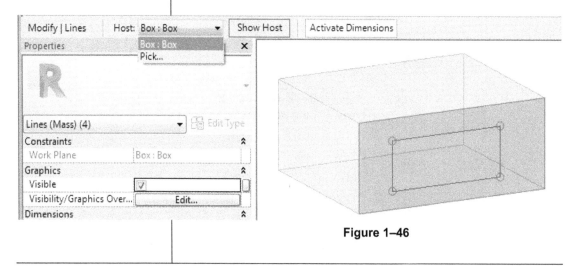

Figure 1–46

Practice 1b | Create Mass Forms

Practice Objectives

- Create an extruded mass form.
- Create a lofted mass form.
- Add a swept void form.

In this practice, you will create two towers in a massing study. For one building, you will extrude a mass form using a simple profile. For the other building, you will create a lofted form using a variety of profiles at different levels and then add a void form using a swept profile, as shown in Figure 1–47.

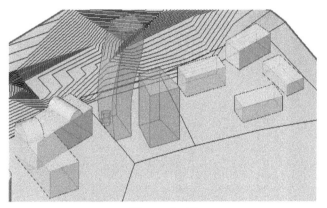

Figure 1–47

Task 1 - Create an Extruded In-Place Mass.

1. In the practice files folder, open **Edmon-Towers-New.rvt**.

2. Open the **Floor Plans: New Site** view. This view displays the new site area, as shown in Figure 1–48.

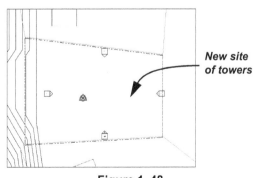

New site of towers

Figure 1–48

3. In the *Massing & Site* tab>Conceptual Mass panel, click (In-Place Mass).

4. In the Name dialog box, enter **Tower-1** and click **OK**.

Add reference planes first if required.

5. In the *Create* tab>Draw panel, click (Model) and then click (Line).

6. In the northwest quadrant of the new site, draw a trapezoid shape that is roughly 80' by 60', as shown in Figure 1–49.

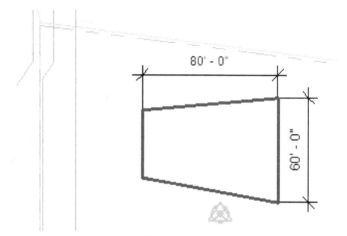

Figure 1–49

7. Open the default 3D view.

8. Select the lines. In the *Modify | Lines* tab>Form panel, click (Create Form). The Autodesk Revit software extrudes the profile to create a solid form.

9. Click on the blue temporary dimension and change it to **140'**.

10. In the *Modify | Form* tab>In-Place Editor panel, click (Finish Mass).

Task 2 - Create Levels.

1. Open the **Elevations (Building Elevation): East** view and zoom in to see the level markers.

2. Set the *elevation* of **Level 2** to **18'**.

3. Set the *name* of the existing **Roof** level to **Level 3**, and its *elevation* to **30'**. Click **Yes** when prompted to rename any corresponding views.

4. Select the newly-named **Level 3**.

5. In the *Modify | Levels* tab>Modify panel, click ⊞ (Array). In the Options Bar, clear the **Group and Associate** option.

6. Create an array of **30 levels**, **12'-0"** apart.

7. Click **Modify** and enter **ZE** to zoom out to the extents of the view.

Task 3 - Create a Lofted In-Place Mass.

1. Return to a 3D view.

2. Create a new In-Place Mass named **Tower-2**.

3. In the *Create* tab>Draw panel, click ⌐ (Model) and then click ▭ (Rectangle).

4. In the Draw panel, click ◈ (Draw on Work Plane).

5. In the Options Bar, verify that *Placement Plane* is set to **Level: Level 1**.

6. Draw a **40'x80'** rectangle south of the first tower.

7. In the Options Bar, change *Placement Plane* to **Level: Level 10**.

8. Draw another rectangle. Use the alignment lines to line up at least one of the sides with the rectangle below. Note that when you hover the cursor over the lines on the active workplane, they highlight.

9. Repeat the process at **Level 20** and **Level 30**, varying the size at each level.

10. Click **Modify** and select the four rectangles.

11. In the *Modify | Lines* tab>Form panel, click 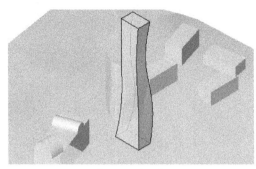 (Create Form). The new tower displays as shown in Figure 1–50. Your design will vary according to the profiles you drew.

Figure 1–50

12. In a plan view, move one or both of the new massing forms so they do not overlap, if required.

13. Do not save the project yet because you want to remain in the same In-Place Mass element.

Task 4 - Add a Void Form.

1. In a 3D view, zoom in to the base of the new tower.

2. Click 〰 (Model) and then select one of the arc drawing tools. In the Options Bar, set the *Placement Plane* to **Level: Level 1**.

3. Draw an arc, as shown in Figure 1–51. This is the path for a sweep. It needs to start outside the existing mass to create the expected void form.

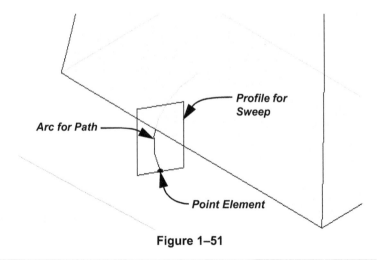

Profile for Sweep

Arc for Path

Point Element

Figure 1–51

4. In the Draw panel, click ⊛ (Point Element).

5. Add a point at one end of the arc if you want to draw a sweep, and at both ends of the arc if you want to draw a swept blend.

6. Click **Modify** and select the Point Element.

7. Draw the profile for the sweep.

8. Repeat the process with the other Point Element if you are creating a swept blend.

9. Click **Modify** and select the path and profile(s).

10. In the Form panel, expand ⌂ (Create Form) and click ⌂ (Void Form).

The new void form is cut out of the existing solid form, as shown in Figure 1–52.

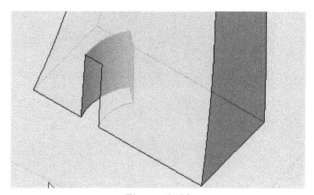

Figure 1–52

11. Click ✓ (Finish Mass).

12. Zoom out to see the entire site with the new towers.

13. Save the project.

1.5 Dynamic Editing for Conceptual Massing

When a completed In-Place Mass element is selected, you can modify the length of its faces by dragging the controls, as shown in Figure 1–53. However, for more precise modification, you can edit the mass in-place, as shown in Figure 1–54.

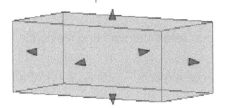

Figure 1–53

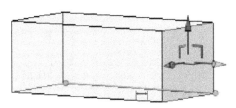

Figure 1–54

- Double-click on an In-Place Mass, or select it and in the

    Modify | Mass tab>Model panel, click 🗔 (Edit In-Place).

In the Edit In-Place mode, you have direct access to the surface, edges, and vertices of a solid or void form, as shown in Figure 1–55. You can quickly and easily manipulate these sub-elements and create new edges and profiles.

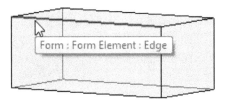

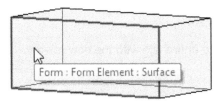

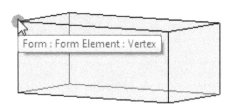

Figure 1–55

- Press <Tab> to cycle between sub-elements as required to select the right one.

Using the 3D Control

When a face, edge, or vertex is selected, the 3D control is displayed.

- To move a selected sub-element directly along an axis, select one of the arrows and drag it in the appropriate direction, as shown in Figure 1–56.

- To move a selected sub-element along a plane (as shown in Figure 1–57), click and drag the plane indicator.

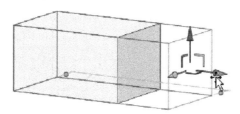 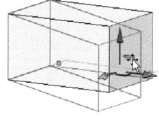

| Figure 1–56 | Figure 1–57 |

Other Modification Options

- You can use ✛ (Move) and ○ (Rotate) when you select a face, an edge, or a vertex. In the example shown in Figure 1–58, the face has been rotated.

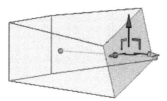

Figure 1–58

- To remove a face, an edge, or a vertex, select it and click

  ✖ (Delete), or press <Delete>. In the example shown in Figure 1–59, a vertex has been selected and deleted.

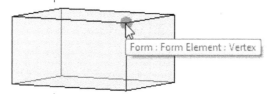 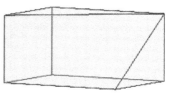

Figure 1–59

- You can lock a mass element so that the profiles in a form work together rather than separately. Select at least one part of the form and, in the *Modify | Form* tab>Form Element panel, click ⬚ (Lock Profiles).

- When you select an edge and the form is not locked, only the selected edge moves, as shown in Figure 1–60. If you lock the form and move the same edge, the entire form based on that profile moves, as shown in Figure 1–61.

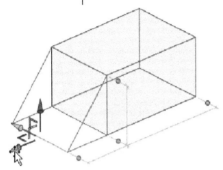
Figure 1–60

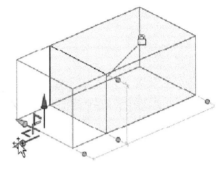
Figure 1–61

- To return the form to its component parts, select the mass element, and in the *Modify | Form* tab>Form Element panel, click ⬚ (Dissolve). Once you have done this, remake the entire form again.

Hint: Use X-Ray to Display a Form's Geometric Framework

Vertices, profiles, and paths do not automatically display while editing forms. In X-Ray mode, the surfaces of a form are transparent and all of the key geometric datums display, as shown in Figure 1–62.

• To enable X-Ray mode, first select a form. Note that you might need to hover the cursor over the edge and press <Tab> until a form has been highlighted. With the form selected, in the *Modify | Form* tab>Form Element panel, click ⏡ (X-Ray).

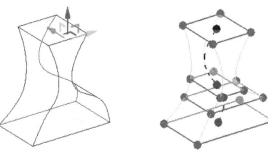

Figure 1–62

• To toggle off X-Ray mode, select the form again and click ⏡ (X-Ray).

• Only one form can have X-Ray mode on at a time.

1.6 Working with Profiles and Edges

While a lot can be done to manipulate mass elements using the dynamic editing tools, there are some additional commands where you can do more precise and complex editing, as shown in Figure 1–63. These include **Edit Profile**, **Add Profile**, **Add Edge**, **Divide Surface**, and **Split Face**.

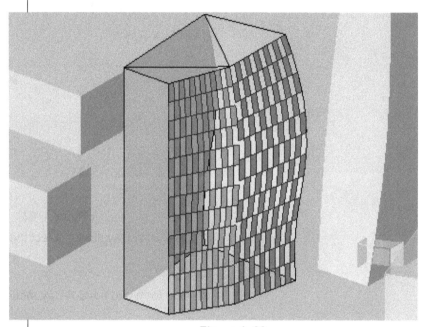

Figure 1–63

Editing Profiles

You can edit the profile or path of a swept form, depending on which edge you selected before starting the editing process.

One option for modifying a form is to edit the profile. For example, you can edit the profile of the bottom outline of an extruded form, as shown in Figure 1–64.

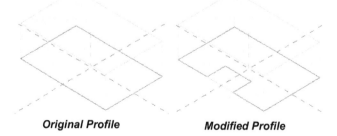

Original Profile　　　　*Modified Profile*

Figure 1–64

How To: Edit Profiles

1. Double-click on the form or select the form or any part of the form and, in the *Modify | Form* tab>Mode panel, click

    (Edit Profile).
2. Pick any profile or path to edit.
3. Sketch mode opens with the profile or path highlighted in magenta. Using the **Draw** and **Modify** tools, make changes as required.

4. Click ✓ (Finish Edit Mode).
5. The selected profile or path is modified.

Adding Edges and Profiles

You can also add edges and profiles to existing forms and then modify the resulting edges, faces, and vertices. An edge can be added to the sides of a form, while a profile can be added along the path of the profile, as shown in Figure 1–65.

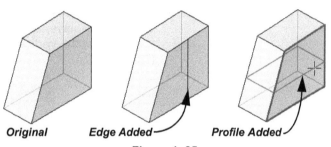

Original　　*Edge Added*　　*Profile Added*

Figure 1–65

Once the edge or profile is placed, you can use the 3D control to create new shapes, as shown in Figure 1–66.

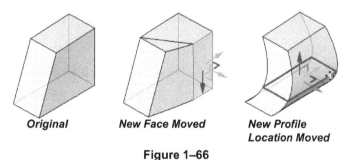

Original　　*New Face Moved*　　*New Profile Location Moved*

Figure 1–66

- If you cannot add an edge to a face, 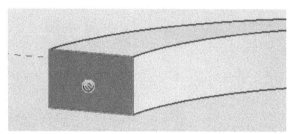 displays, as shown in Figure 1–67.

Figure 1–67

How To: Add an Edge

1. Select anywhere on the form.
2. In the *Modify | Form* tab>Form Element panel, click ⌂⁺ (Add Edge) or right-click and select **Add Edge**.
3. Hover the cursor over a face. A new edge that reflects the geometry displays, as shown in Figure 1–68. Alternately, pick two points at the vertices or edges of a face, as shown in Figure 1–69.

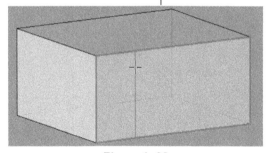

Figure 1–68

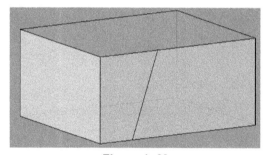

Figure 1–69

How To: Add a Profile

1. Select anywhere on the form.
2. In the *Modify | Form* tab>Form Element panel, click ⌂⁺ (Add Profile) or right-click and select **Add Profile**.

3. A new profile displays on the selected form when the cursor is moved onto and follows it.

- The profile automatically adjusts its shape to match the exterior of the form wherever the cursor is located, as shown in Figure 1–70.

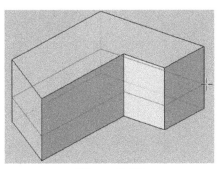

Figure 1–70

4. Click to place the new profile.

Modifying the Faces of Mass Elements

Mass faces can be modified to show patterns and materials. You can apply a pattern similar to creating a curtain wall layout using the **Divide Surface** option, as shown on the top of the mass element in Figure 1–71. You can also split a face into separate surfaces so you can apply different materials to each part, as shown on the base of the mass element in Figure 1–71.

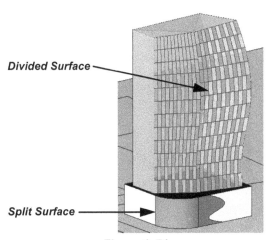

Divided Surface

Split Surface

Figure 1–71

How To: Divide and Pattern a Mass Face

1. Select the face of a mass element.
2. In the *Modify | Form* tab>Divide panel, click 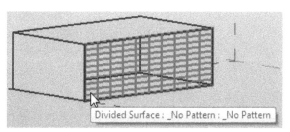 (Divide Surface).
3. The surface is divided using a basic U-V Grid, as shown in Figure 1–72.

Divided Surface : _No Pattern : _No Pattern

Figure 1–72

4. In the Type Selector, select a pattern from the patterns available, as shown in Figure 1–73.
5. In the Options Bar or Properties (as shown in Figure 1–74), modify the U-V Grid layout.

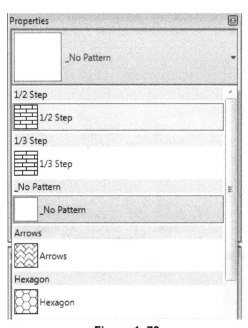

Figure 1–73

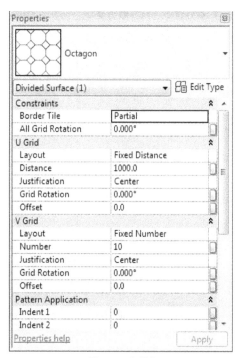

Figure 1–74

6. In the *Modify | Divide Surface* tab>contextual panels (shown in Figure 1–75), you can further modify and display the patterns.

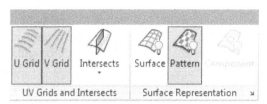

Figure 1–75

How To: Split Mass Faces

1. In the *Modify* tab>Geometry panel, click 🗐 (Split Face).
2. Select the face of the mass element you want to modify.
3. In the *Modify* tab>Draw panel, use the sketch tools to create a sketch as required, to define the split, as shown in Figure 1–76.

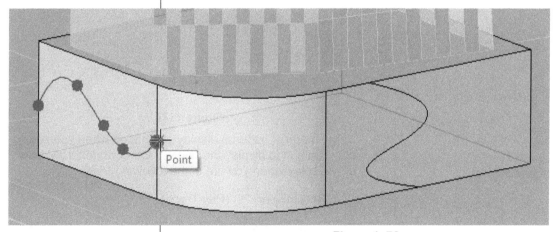

Figure 1–76

- Splitting faces does not create an additional face but you can modify the material in each area.

- The sketch that defines the split must be a closed shape completely inside the face or an open shape that touches the face edges.

- You can split the face of an In-Place Mass either directly on the face (without entering the mass) or in the In-Place Edit mode.

How To: Add Materials to Individual Mass Faces

1. In the *Modify* tab>Geometry panel, click 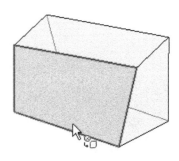 (Paint).
2. Select a material in the Material Browser, as shown on the left in Figure 1–77.
3. Select the face(s) of the mass that you want to paint, as shown on the right in Figure 1–77.

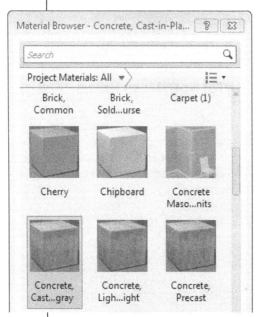

Figure 1–77

- Some material patterns display as shaded when you zoom out. Zoom in to display the pattern. Other material patterns only display when you are in the following Visual Styles:

  (Realistic) or (Ray Trace).

- To change the material applied to a face, in the *Modify* tab> Geometry panel, expand (Paint) and click (Remove Paint). Select the face(s) from which you want to remove the material.

- Older versions of materials may need to be updated with appearance assets. All legacy materials still work but they may not be as complex and nuanced when rendering.

Practice 1c | Modify In-Place Masses

Practice Objectives

- Modify mass elements.
- Add new profiles and edges.
- Modify faces by dividing or splitting them.

In this practice, you will manipulate the vertices, faces, and edges of an extruded In-Place Mass element using the 3D control. You will also add profiles and an edge. An example of a possible outcome is shown in Figure 1–78. Additionally, you will divide a face, apply a pattern, split another face, and then paint them with a material.

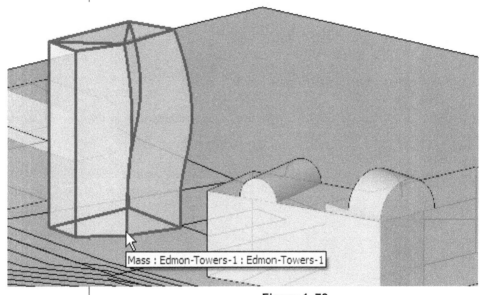

Figure 1–78

Task 1 - Modify an In-Place Mass.

1. In the practice files folder, open **Edmon-Towers-Modify.rvt**.

2. Select the taller mass of **Tower-2** and temporarily hide it.

3. Orient the 3D view so you can see the **Tower-1** extruded mass element.

4. Click on the mass element and modify it slightly using the controls, as shown in Figure 1–79. You can make minor modifications to an In-Place Mass without editing the entire mass form.

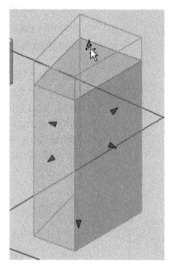

Figure 1–79

5. With the mass still selected, in the *Modify | Mass* tab>Model panel, click 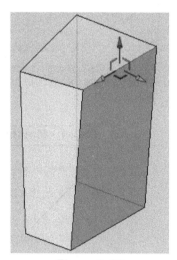 (Edit In-Place).

6. Select one of the edges and modify it slightly using the 3D control, similar to that shown in Figure 1–80.

Figure 1–80

Task 2 - Add and modify profiles and an edge.

1. Select an element in the form.

2. In the *Modify | Form* tab>Form Element panel, click ⬡ (X-Ray).

3. In the Form Element panel, click ⬡ (Add Profile).

4. Add a profile about one quarter of the way up the form.

5. Repeat this process to add two more profiles, so that the form is divided into four sections, as shown in Figure 1–81.

Do not worry about placing the profiles exactly. Their locations can be adjusted later.

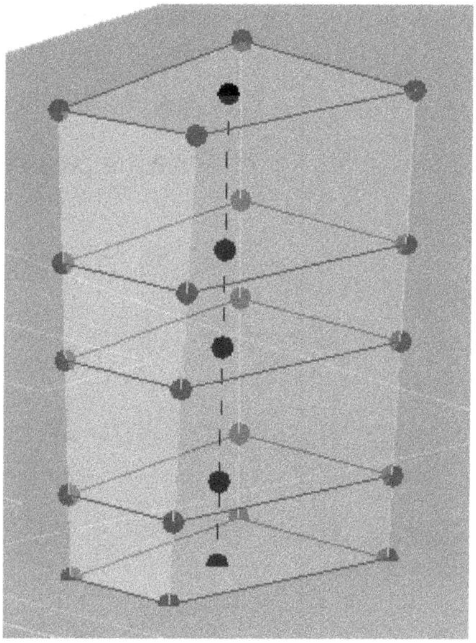

Figure 1–81

6. Use ⬡ (Add Edge) to add an edge to one side of the building.

7. Select the new face and move it out sightly using the 3D control.

8. Manipulate the various vertices and edges to reshape the mass.

9. Toggle off X-ray mode.

Task 3 - Divide and Pattern Surfaces.

1. Select one of the mass faces.

2. In the *Modify | Form* tab>Divide panel, click (Divide Surface)

3. In the Type Selector, select a pattern.

4. Modify the pattern properties using tools in the ribbon and Options bar.

5. (Optional). Select a different face and use (Split Face) and (Paint) to apply materials.

6. Click (Finish Mass).

7. Save the project.

1.7 Moving from Massing to Building

When you have established a massing study, you can start the design development with walls, etc., you do not have to start over. Instead, you can use tools in the Autodesk Revit software to create walls, floors, roofs, and curtain systems from the faces of the masses in the project as shown in Figure 1–82.

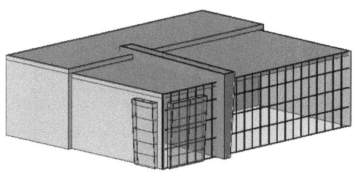

Figure 1–82

- Some elements in your building must be created with mass elements. For example, if you want to have sloping walls or curtain walls you need to create a mass element to host them.

- You can add walls, floors, roofs, and curtain systems to the faces of mass elements using the **Wall**, **Roof**, and **Floor** commands in the *Architecture* tab>Build panel. For example, when you start the **Wall** command, you can click (Pick Faces) as the drawing method, as shown in Figure 1–83.

Figure 1–83

- You can also use the specific commands found in the *Massing & Site* tab>Model by Face panel, as shown in Figure 1–84.

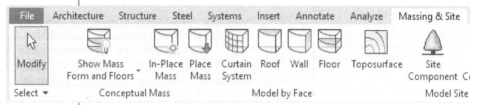

Figure 1–84

How To: Use the Model by Face Tools

1. Open a view where the mass faces display and where you want to apply the building elements. This can be done in either a 3D or elevation view.

2. In the *Massing & Site* tab>Model by Face panel, click  (Curtain System), ⬒ (Roof), ⬒ (Wall), or ⬒ (Floor).

3. In the Type Selector, select an element type.
4. Select the faces you want to turn into elements.
5. In the contextual tab>Multiple Selection panel, click the related **Create** command.

Wall by Face Options

Location Line is grayed out if a curtain wall style is selected.

- Ensure that the *Location Line value* is set to **Core Face: Exterior**. This keeps the walls on the inside of the mass.

- You can create walls on sloped faces using this tool.

Curtain Systems Options

A Curtain System is a type of curtain wall that is typically on a curved or angled face.

- In the *Modify | Place Curtain System by Face* tab>Multiple Selection panel, verify that ⬚ (Select Multiple) is highlighted if you are planning to select more than one face for a curtain system at a time.

Roof by Face Options

- After you have created a roof by face, you can use shape handles to modify the overhang of the roof as shown in Figure 1–85.

The overhang distance is remembered if you change the mass.

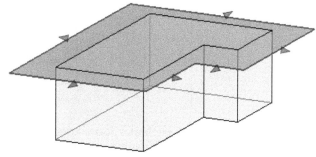

Figure 1–85

Creating Floors from Mass Elements

To create floors in a massing study, you must first create Mass Floors. These are the basis for creating floors and also help track the floor area of the building. Once you have the mass floors in a project, you can click 🗑 (Floor by Face) to add the floor elements on the faces.

How To: Create Mass Floors

1. Select a mass.
2. In the *Modify | Mass* tab>Model panel, click 🗑 (Mass Floors).
3. In the Mass Floors dialog box, select the levels where you want floor area faces to be located, as shown in Figure 1–86, and click **OK**.

If you have a lot of levels to select hold the <Ctrl> or <Shift> key to select multiple.

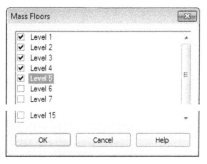

Figure 1–86

The mass floors display in the massing study, as shown in Figure 1–87.

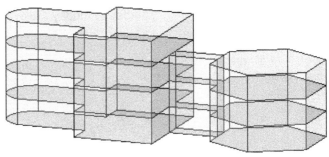

Figure 1–87

- Mass floors keep track of the area, exterior surface area, volume, and perimeter of each floor. This information can be used in schedules and tags.

Hint: Updating Elements Connected to Mass Elements

Elements applied to mass elements, such as walls, floors, roofs, and curtain systems do not automatically update when the massing element changes as shown on the left in Figure 1–88. Select the mass element and in the *Modify | Mass* tab>Model panel, click 🗔 (Related Hosts). Then in the *Modify | Multi-Select* tab>Model by Face panel, click 🗔 (Update to Face). The elements update, as shown on the right in Figure 1–88.

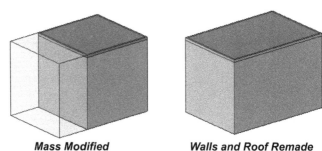

Mass Modified   *Walls and Roof Remade*

Figure 1–88

- If you only want to update one element (such as a roof), select the element that is hosted by the mass and in the *Modify | <element type>* tab>Model by Face panel, click 🗔 (Update to Face). Note that the icon varies according to the element type selected.

Practice 1d | Move From Massing to Building

Practice Objectives

- Add mass floors.
- Use existing schedules to track the coverage of the site and the gross area of the mass, while making changes to one of the towers
- Add walls, floors, roofs, and curtain systems to the finished mass towers.

In this practice, you will add mass floors to specified levels and investigate the site coverage and building volume, as shown in Figure 1–89. You will also add walls, floors, curtain systems, and roofs to the faces of the Conceptual Mass elements.

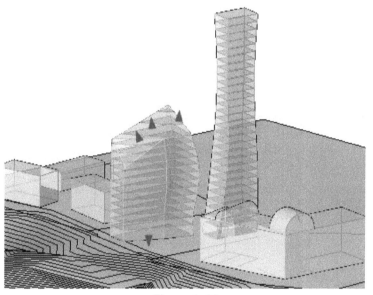

Figure 1–89

Task 1 - Add Massing Floors.

1. In the practice files folder, open **Edmon-Towers-Building.rvt**.

2. Select the two curved masses included in the project.

3. In the *Modify | Mass* tab>Model panel, click ⛃ (Mass Floors).

Some levels are higher than the current height of the masses, By selecting them now, they will automatically be applied when the height of the masses is changed.

4. Select all of the levels in the Mass Floors dialog box and click **OK**. The new mass floors display as shown in Figure 1–90.

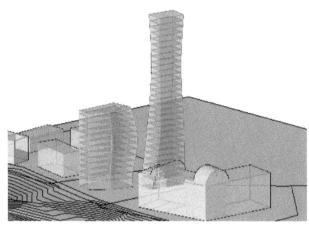

Figure 1–90

Task 2 - Track Site Coverage and Gross Area Using Schedules.

---

1. Close any other projects and in the Quick Access Toolbar, click ⬚ (Close Hidden) to close any windows that do no need to be open.

2. Open the following four views on your screen:
   - *3D Views:* **Site View**
   - *Floor Plans:* **New Site**
   - *Schedules/Quantities:* **Building Volume Schedule**
   - *Schedules/Quantities:* **Coverage of Site**

- The **Coverage of Site** schedule enables you to track how much of the site that the proposed building covers. It lists the actual and maximum footprints in both square feet and percentage. You can enter the actual site area in the *Parcel* column and the amount of the site that the building is permitted to cover in the *Max Footprint (%)* column. The Autodesk Revit software does the rest.

- **Building Volume Schedule** displays the Total Floor Area and Total Floor Volume at the bottom of the schedule. If the zoning restrictions or program requirements limit the overall floor area of the building, the schedule tracks this for you.

3. Return to the 3D view and type **WT** (Window Tile) so that all four views display.

4. Type **ZA** (Zoom All) to display the entire 3D view and the New Site plan.

5. Click in the **New Site** view and select the Property Line, as shown in Figure 1–91.

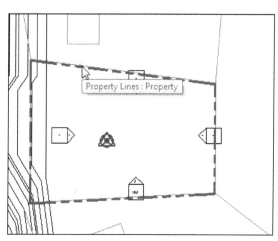

Figure 1–91

6. In Properties, the *Area* is **43298.77SF**. This is the size you use for the *Parcel* column.

7. In the **Coverage of Site** schedule, enter **43299** in the *Parcel* cell and **20** in the *Max Footprint (%)* cell, as shown in Figure 1–92.

<Coverage of Site>				
A	B	C	D	E
Parcel	Actual Footprint	Max Footprint	Current Footprint (%)	Max Footprint (%)
43,299 SF	8,263 SF	8,660	19.1	20

Figure 1–92

8. Based on initial numbers in the **Coverage of Site** schedule, both towers are within the *Max Footprint*.

9. Select one of the tower masses. Use the shape handles to change the height and shape of the mass. Watch the schedules to ensure that the *Current Footprint* value remains below 20% and the *Floor Area* total remains below 130,000 SF.

10. If you have time, you can also modify the masses using **Edit In-Place**.

11. Save the project.

Task 3 - Add Walls, Floors, Roofs, and Curtain Systems.

1. Expand the 3D view.

2. Zoom in on one of the mass elements.

3. In the *Massing & Site* tab>Model by Face panel, click
   (Floor).

4. Select the floors and click (Create Floor).

5. Repeat the process with Walls, Roofs, and Curtain Systems.

6. Save the project.

Chapter Review Questions

1. Mass elements print by default when you place the view on a sheet.

   a. True

   b. False

2. Which of the following elements was NOT created using the basic family types that come with the Autodesk Revit software?

   a.

   b.

   c.

   d.

3. What element(s) need to be placed first to create a blended sweep form?

   a. Two profiles on different work planes.

   b. A profile on an extrusion.

   c. More than two profiles on different levels.

   d. Two or more existing forms.

4. How do you cut a portion out of a Conceptual Mass element, as shown in Figure 1–93?

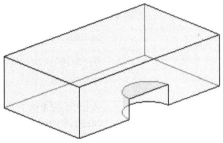

Figure 1–93

a. Select the form and click 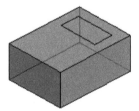 (Edit Profile).

b. Create a void form in the mass element.

c. Create another mass element and use ⌀ (Cut Geometry).

d. Edit the form and add another profile to it.

5. Which of the mass form types is created from three or more profiles?

a. Sweep

b. Swept Blend

c. Loft

d. Extrusion

6. The start of a mass form is a sketch. How do you place a sketch on another form, as shown in Figure 1–94? Select the **Draw** tool that you want to use and then...

Figure 1–94

a. Use the **Draw on Face** tool.

b. Use the **Draw on Work Plane** tool.

c. Set the *Placement Plane* to a **Level**.

7. How do you move a sketch from one plane to another plane, as shown in Figure 1–95?

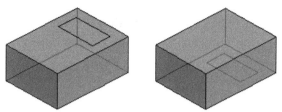

Figure 1–95

   a. Change the *Placement Plane*.

   b. Use the **Move** command.

   c. Change the *Host*.

   d. Use the **Align** command.

8. What must be in place before you can add a floor to a mass element, as shown in Figure 1–96?

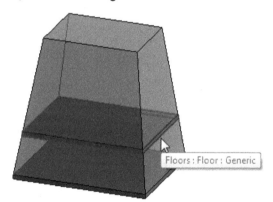

Floors : Floor : Generic

Figure 1–96

   a. Additional mass elements at each floor.

   b. Sketches for each floor.

   c. An additional floor parameter in Properties.

   d. Mass floor elements at each floor.

Command Summary

Button	Command	Location
	Cut Geometry	• **Ribbon:** *Modify* tab>Geometry panel
	Edit In-Place	• **Ribbon:** *Modify | Mass* tab>Model panel
	Edit Work Plane	• **Ribbon:** *Modify | Mass* tab>Work Plane panel
	In-Place Mass	• **Ribbon:** *Massing & Site* tab> Conceptual Mass panel
	Load Family	• **Ribbon:** *Modify | Place Mass* tab> Mode panel
	Paint	• **Ribbon:** *Modify* tab>Geometry panel
	Place Mass	• **Ribbon:** *Massing & Site* tab> Conceptual Mass panel
	Place on Face	• **Ribbon:** *Modify | Place Mass* tab> Placement panel
	Place on Work Plane	• **Ribbon:** *Modify | Place Mass* tab> Placement panel
	Show Mass by Form and Floors	• **Ribbon:** *Massing & Site* tab> Conceptual Mass panel expand Show Mass
	Show Mass by View Settings	• **Ribbon:** *Massing & Site* tab> Conceptual Mass panel expand Show Mass

Conceptual Mass Environment

Button	Command	Location
	Add Edge	• **Ribbon:** *Modify | Form* tab>Form Element panel • **Right-click:** Add Edge
	Add Profile	• **Ribbon:** *Modify | Form* tab>Form Element panel • **Right-click:** Add Profile
	Create Form	• **Ribbon:** *Modify | Place Lines* tab> Form panel
	Divide Surface	• **Ribbon:** *Modify | Form* tab>Divide panel
	Draw on Face	• **Ribbon:** *Modify | Place Lines* tab> Draw panel
	Draw on Work Plane	• **Ribbon:** *Modify | Place Lines* tab> Draw panel
	Point Element	• **Ribbon:** *Modify | Place Lines* tab> Draw panel
	Model Line	• **Ribbon:** *Modify | Form* tab>Draw panel

	Reference Line	• **Ribbon:** *Modify*	*Form* tab>Draw panel
	Reference Plane	• **Ribbon:** *Modify*	*Form* tab>Draw panel
	X-Ray	• **Ribbon:** *Modify*	*Form* tab>Form Element panel • **Right-click:** X-Ray
	Void Form	• **Ribbon:** *Modify*	*Lines* tab>Form panel>expand Create Form

From Massing to Building

	Floor (by Face)	• **Ribbon:** *Massing & Site* tab>Model by Face panel
	Curtain System (by Face)	• **Ribbon:** *Massing & Site* tab>Model by Face panel
	Mass Floors	• **Ribbon:** *Modify*	*Mass* tab>Model panel
	Related Hosts	• **Ribbon:** *Modify*	*Mass* tab>Model panel
	Roof (by Face)	• **Ribbon:** *Massing & Site* tab>Model by Face panel
	Wall (by Face)	• **Ribbon:** *Massing & Site* tab>Model by Face panel
	Update to Face	• **Ribbon:** *Modify*	*Multi-Select* tab> Model by Face panel

Space Planning and Area Analysis

Space planning using rooms and areas can be used in conceptual design and as part of the Building Information Model. The tools that come with Autodesk® Revit® are very powerful and enable you to layout rooms in a building, and track room information through all of the phases of a project. If you are working with rentable spaces, you can also add similar elements that keep track of the areas in a project. Both rooms and areas can have customized views that use color schemes that show the information graphically.

Learning Objectives in this Chapter

- Add rooms, room boundaries, and room tags to a project.
- Create area plans.
- Place area boundaries and areas.
- Set up a color scheme in a view.
- Define new color schemes by value and by range.

2.1 Space Planning

The Room element is a powerful tool in the Autodesk® Revit® software. With this element, you can set up information to use in schedules and color diagrams to help present data or do take-offs. They also contain area, perimeter, and volume information about each room as well as the room name and number, as shown in Figure 2–1.

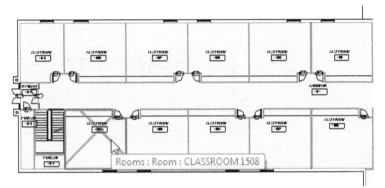

Figure 2–1

- Most walls, roofs, floors, ceilings, columns, and curtain systems are *Room Bounding* elements. One exception is the retaining wall type, which typically does not enclose rooms.

- You can add room separation lines to create rooms that are not bounded by walls.

- You can place room elements without any original bounding elements. They expand to fit any boundary that later encloses them.

How To: Create Rooms in a Plan

1. Draw the walls and other bounding elements that you want to have in your building.

2. In the *Architecture* tab>Room & Area panel, click ⬛ (Room) or enter **RM**.

3. In the *Modify | Place Room* tab>Tag panel, click 🏷 (Tag on Placement) if you want to include a tag as you place the room.

4. Use the Options Bar (shown in Figure 2–2) to:
   - Set the *Upper Limit* and *Offset*.
   - Set the *Orientation* of the tag and the *Leader*.
   - Select a *Room* name from the drop-down list (if room names have been previously created in a schedule).

| Modify \| Place Room | Upper Limit: | Level 1 ▼ | Offset: 10' 0" | 🔲 Horizontal ▼ | ☐ Leader Room: New | ▼ |

Figure 2–2

5. Move the cursor into a boundary area and click to place the room, as shown in Figure 2–3. Or, in the *Modify | Place Room* tab>Room panel, click ⬕ (Place Rooms Automatically) to add rooms to every bounding area.

Select one room and set the first number before placing rooms automatically so they will increment as expected.

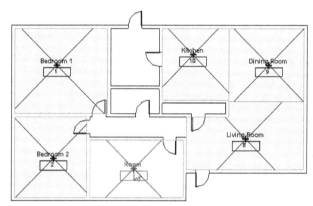

Figure 2–3

6. Continue adding rooms.

   - In the *Modify | Place Room* tab>Room panel, click ▢ (Highlight Boundaries) to display all of the bounding objects in the project in orange. An alert box displays a warning that the room bounding elements are highlighted. When you close the alert box, it toggles off the highlighting of the bounding objects.

Hint: Setting up Views to Show Rooms

Rooms do not display in views by default, so it can help to create views specifically for rooms. To do this, duplicate an existing plan or elevation view. Then, in the Visibility/Graphic Overrides dialog box, in the *Model* tab, toggle on **Rooms> Interior Fill** and/or **Reference** to show the crossing lines.

Room Separation Boundaries

Boundaries for rooms can also be defined by room separation lines. Use these where you might not have a wall to separate the areas, but still want to specify them as different rooms. For example, in a house you can have a kitchen, dining area, and living area in a larger room that is not separated by walls, as shown in Figure 2–4.

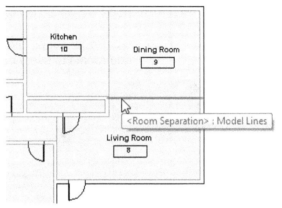

Figure 2–4

How To: Create Room Separation Boundaries

1. In the *Architecture* tab>Room & Area panel, click ⬚ (Room Separator).
2. In the *Modify | Place Room Separation* tab>Draw panel, use the sketch tools to draw the edges of the boundary.

3. Use ⬚ (Room) to add rooms in the areas bounded by the separation lines.

• You can edit room separation lines by splitting, trimming, etc.

Modifying Rooms

To select a room, hover the cursor over it until you see the crossing mark, as shown in Figure 2–5. Then, select one of the reference lines to select the room.

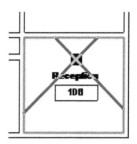

Figure 2–5

- When a room is selected, you can modify its Properties, as shown in Figure 2–6.

You can select several rooms at once to add the same information to all of them.

Rooms (1)	▼	🔲 Edit Type
Constraints		✕ ▲
Level	Level 1	
Upper Limit	Level 1	
Limit Offset	10' 0"	
Base Offset	0' 0"	
Dimensions		✕
Area	482.61 SF	
Perimeter	88' 4"	
Unbounded Height	10' 0"	
Volume	Not Computed	
Computation Height	0' 0"	
Identity Data		✕
Number	2	
Name	Room	
Image		▼

Figure 2–6

- You can also modify the vertical height of rooms in sections by using controls, as shown in Figure 2–7, or temporary dimensions.

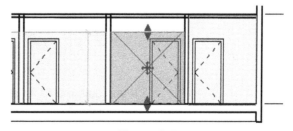

Figure 2–7

Adding Room Tags

The Room Tag command is separate from other tag commands.

Room Tags can be added during or after rooms are added to a project. There are three room tag types: **Room Tag**, **Room Tag With Area**, and **Room Tag With Volume**, as shown in Figure 2–8.

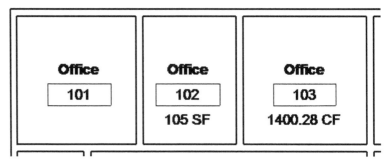

Figure 2–8

How To: Place a Room Tag

1. Place rooms without tags in the project.
2. In the *Architecture* tab>Room & Area panel, click ▣ (Tag Room) or in the *Annotate* tab>Tag panel, click ▣ (Room Tag) or enter **RT**.
3. In Properties, select the tag type.
4. Click in the room you want to tag and repeat to tag as many rooms as required.

• Rooms can be tagged in plan or section views.

• Rooms can be tagged using ▣ (Tag all Not Tagged).

• To change the room name or number, select the tag and click on the name or number to modify it, as shown in Figure 2–9.

Figure 2–9

• If you delete a room tag, the room is not deleted. However, when you delete a room, the tag is deleted as well.

- If you select a tag, you can modify the *Orientation* and add or remove a *Leader* in the Options Bar, as shown in Figure 2–10.

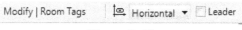

Figure 2–10

- If you move a tag outside its room without a leader, it loses the association, as shown in Figure 2–11. You can add a leader or move it back in the room to re-associate it.

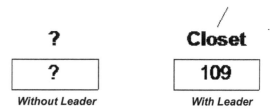

?	**Closet**
?	**109**
Without Leader	*With Leader*

Figure 2–11

Room Schedules

Room schedules are used to keep track of data included in a room, such as the name, number, occupancy, and finishes. In the schedule you can select multiple rooms and apply the same information to them all.

- Room schedules can include standard building components, such as the room schedule shown in Figure 2–12.

<Room Schedule>			
A	B	C	D
Number	Name	Department	Room Style
101	Office	Sales	Office-Standard
102	Office	Sales	Office-Standard
103	Workroom	Sales	Workroom
104	Office	Accounting	Office-Standard
105	Office	Accounting	Office-Standard
106	Office	Accounting	Office-Standard
107	Reception	Acoounting	Reception
108	Office	Accounting	Office-Executive

Typical Room Schedule

Figure 2–12

Key schedules, such as the Finish Schedule shown in Figure 2–13, are also created from rooms.

<Finish Schedule>				
A	B	C	D	E
Key Name	Base Finish	Floor Finish	Wall Finish	Ceiling Finish
Corridor	Vinyl	Carpet	Painted	Ceiling Tile
Office-Executive	Wood	Wood	Painted	Ceiling Tile
Office-Standard	Vinyl	Carpet	Painted	Ceiling Tile
Reception	Vinyl	Carpet	Painted	Ceiling Tile
Workroom	Vinyl	Tile	Painted	Ceiling Tile

Typical Finish Schedule (Key Schedule)

Figure 2–13

Room Settings

You can set the way the Autodesk Revit software calculates volumes and boundary locations. In the *Architecture* tab>Room & Area panel, expand the panel title and click (Area and Volume Computations) to open the dialog box, as shown in Figure 2–14.

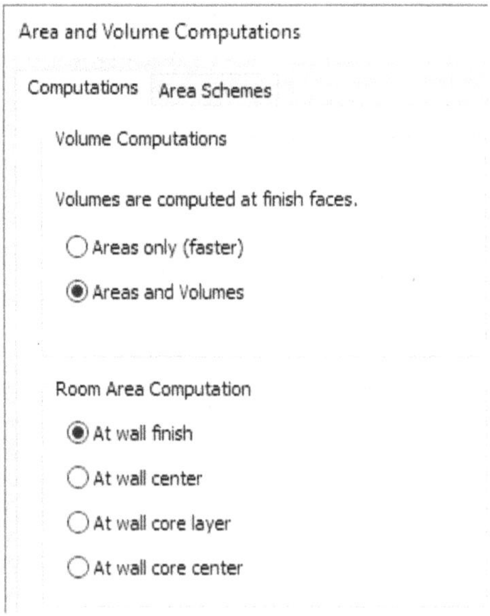

Figure 2–14

- Calculating volumes slows down the speed of working in a project. You might only want to toggle it on before you do an evaluation.

Practice 2a

Space Planning

Practice Objectives

- Set up a view that displays rooms.
- Add rooms and room separation lines to a project.
- Review a room schedule.

In this practice, you will set up a view that displays rooms, add rooms, room separation lines, and room tags to an existing project. You will modify the room tags and give each room a name, as shown in Figure 2–15. Finally, you will review a Room Schedule and modify some of the contents.

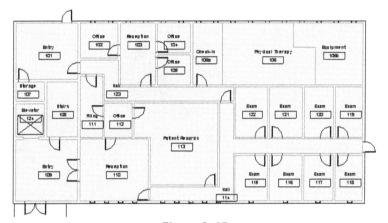

Figure 2–15

Task 1 - Create a view and add rooms.

1. In the practice files folder, open **Medical-Office-Rooms.rvt**.

2. Duplicate the **Floor Plans: Level 1** view and rename it **Level 1 - Rooms**.

3. Open the Visibility/Graphic Overrides dialog box.

4. In the *Model Categories* tab, expand *Rooms* and select **Interior Fill**. Click **OK**.

5. In the *Architecture* tab>Room & Area panel, click ⬚ (Room) or enter **RM**. Verify that ⌐① (Tag on Placement) is on.

6. Place the first room in the upper left corner of the building.

7. Zoom in on the room and select the number in the room tag. Change the tag's room number to **101**. This causes the rest of the tags to automatically increment based on this number.

8. Start the **Room** command again.

    *   To control the order of the room numbers, click in each room.
    *   If the room number order does not matter, click 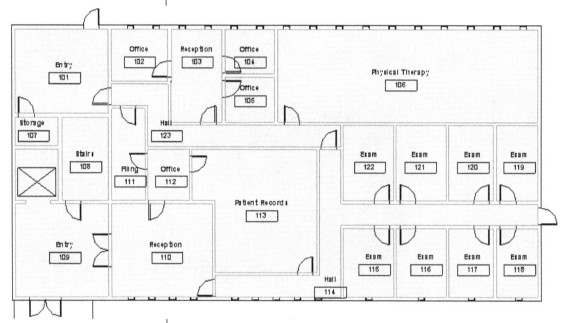 (Place Rooms Automatically).
    *   Do not change the room names as you place them.

9. After you have placed all of the rooms, zoom in and start naming them, as shown in Figure 2–16.

Figure 2–16

*   To modify one room name at a time, click on the room tag and set a new name.
*   To modify several rooms that need the same name, select the room elements and, in *Properties,* enter the name for the selected set of tags.

10. Save the project.

Task 2 - Add room separation lines.

1. In the *Architecture* tab>Room & Area panel, click 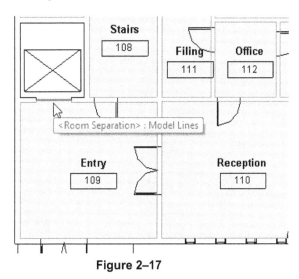 (Room Separator).

2. Draw a line across the opening at the elevator. The Entry room remains, but the elevator area does not have a room, as shown in Figure 2–17.

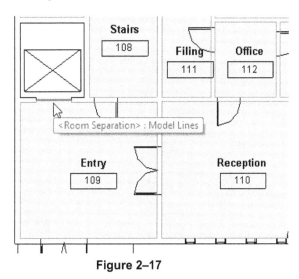

Figure 2–17

3. Add a room and name it **Elevator**.

4. In the large room in the upper right corner, use room separation lines to divide the area, as shown in Figure 2–18. Add rooms to the new spaces and modify the room tag names and numbers.

The room number might be different in your drawing.

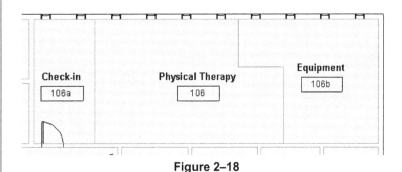

Figure 2–18

5. Save the project.

Task 3 - Review a room schedule.

1. In the Project Browser, expand the **Schedule/Quantities** node and select **Room Schedule**. The list of rooms displays, as shown in Figure 2–19.

    - Your room names might be associated with different numbers.

\<Room Schedule\>				
A	B	C	D	E
Number	Name	Area	Department	Occupancy
101	Entry	277 SF		
102	Office	105 SF		
103	Reception	169 SF		
104	Office	77 SF		
105	Office	77 SF		
106	Physical Therapy	420 SF		
106a	Check-in	149 SF		
106b	Equipment	279 SF		
107	Storage	44 SF		
108	Stairs	135 SF		

Figure 2–19

2. Add information to the *Department* and *Occupancy* columns for individual rooms or groups of rooms.

3. Save and close the project.

2.2 Area Analysis

Rooms calculate areas based on walls and other room bounding elements. However, you might need to define areas that extend across a variety of rooms. In addition, if you are working in a leasing situation, you might need to work with standard building rentable area definitions, as shown in Figure 2–20.

The Area Analysis tools in the Autodesk Revit software can accomplish these and related tasks. Many of the processes for area analysis are similar to those for rooms, such as defining boundaries, adding tags, and creating schedules.

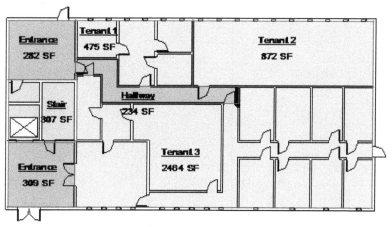

Figure 2–20

Creating Area Plans

You must create an area plan before you can use the Area tools. The plan can provide the overall area of the building footprint, as shown in Figure 2–21 with the heavy lines or it can be subdivided into additional areas.

Automatic boundary lines for Rentable space are on the inside of the exterior walls. For Gross Building area plans, the boundary lines are on the outside of the exterior walls.

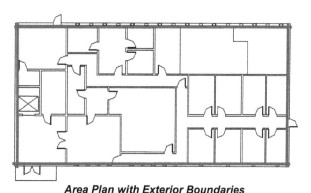

Area Plan with Exterior Boundaries
Figure 2–21

How To: Create an Area Plan

1. In the *Architecture* tab>Room & Area panel, expand  (Area) and click (Area Plan).
2. In the New Area Plan dialog box, in the *Type* list, select the type of area plan that you want to create, as shown in Figure 2–22. The standard templates include two types: **Rentable** and **Gross Building**.

Figure 2–22

- If the **Do not duplicate existing views** option is selected, additional area plans cannot be created where some exist.

3. Select the level(s) from which you want to create area plan views.
4. Click **OK**.
5. An alert box opens, prompting you to create boundary lines associated with external walls, as shown in Figure 2–23. Click **Yes**.

If you do not automatically create boundary lines around the external walls, you need to add them later.

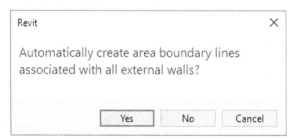

Figure 2–23

• Area plans are created for the selected levels. Each area plan is a separate view. They are listed in the Project Browser in the *Area Plans* area and divided by type, as shown in Figure 2–24.

Figure 2–24

Placing Area Boundaries

The area's type controls the precise location of boundary lines with respect to the walls. For a description of the area measurement rules for each area type, see the Autodesk Revit Help files.

The next step in creating an area analysis is to add *area boundary* lines in the area plan to define sections of the building, such as offices, stores, and common areas, as shown in Figure 2–25.

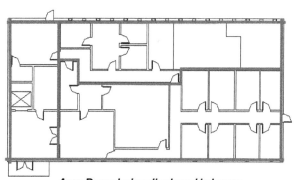

Area Boundaries displayed in heavy

Figure 2–25

• Area boundaries display in a blue/purple line color.

• Gross Building area plans automatically include the area element.

How To: Create an Area Boundary

1. Open the Area Plan you want to work in.
2. In the *Architecture* tab>Room & Area panel, click ⊠ (Area Boundary).
3. In the Options Bar, select **Apply Area Rules** so that the boundary lines will move to the face or center of the walls according to the type of area you specify later.
4. In the *Modify | Place Area Boundary* tab>Draw panel, use the sketch tools to draw the boundaries or select walls to specify them. Use the modify tools, such as **Trim/Extend to Corner**, as required.

Adding Areas

Once you have created the area plan and added boundaries to separate areas, you are ready to add area elements, as shown in Figure 2–26. These elements are similar to rooms in that they include much more than just a name for the area.

Office

482 SF

Office

606 SF

<Area Boundary> : Model Lines

Figure 2–26

* To have the area background display, in the Visibility/Graphic Overrides dialog box, expand *Areas* and select **Color Fill**.

* Area information can be displayed in Gross Area or Rentable Area Schedules that include the area, name, type, and other options.

How To: Add Areas

1. In the *Architecture* tab>Room & Area panel, expand ⊠ (Area) and click ⊠ (Area).
2. Move the cursor over the closed area boundaries on the area plan to highlight the area. Click to place the area within the boundary. You can specify tags for the areas as you go.
3. Continue placing areas as required.

- When you select one or more area elements, you can set the *Area Type* in Properties, as shown in Figure 2–27. Items that are grayed out (such as the *Area* and *Perimeter*) are automatically updated.

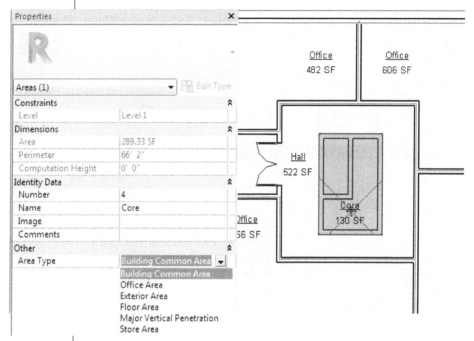

Figure 2–27

- Area types include **Building Common**, **Office Area**, **Exterior Area** (such as a patio or balcony), **Floor Area** (utility rooms and corridors), **Major Vertical Penetration**, and **Store Area** (retail), as shown in Figure 2–27.

- Modifying the area boundaries or associated walls changes the calculated area in the tag.

- In the *Architecture* tab>Room & Area panel, click ⊠ (Tag Area) if you need to add area tags later.

- You can also use 🗖 (Tag All Not Tagged).

How To: Create Area Schemes

1. In the *Architecture* tab>Room & Area panel, expand the panel title and click (Area and Volume Computations).
2. In the dialog box, select the *Area Schemes* tab.
3. Click **New** to add a new scheme, as shown in Figure 2–28.

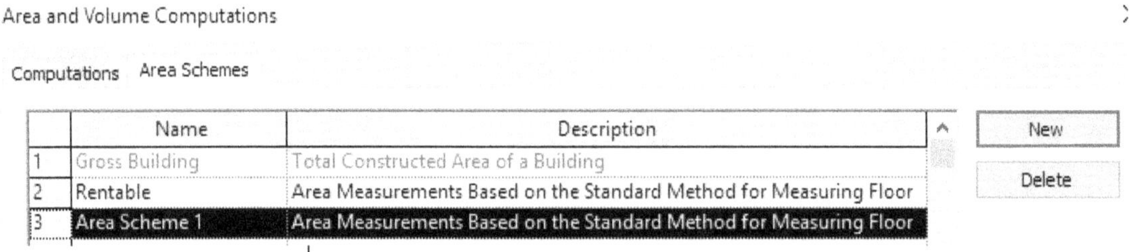

Area and Volume Computations

Computations   Area Schemes

	Name	Description		
1	Gross Building	Total Constructed Area of a Building		New
2	Rentable	Area Measurements Based on the Standard Method for Measuring Floor		Delete
3	Area Scheme 1	Area Measurements Based on the Standard Method for Measuring Floor		

Figure 2–28

4. Rename the scheme and add a description.

•   New schemes use the same area types as the rentable scheme, and include settings for area calculations and various area boundary locations. These are used in the color schemes.

Practice 2b | Area Analysis

Practice Objectives

- Create a gross area plan and a rentable area plan.
- Modify area types in a schedule.
- Place plans and schedules on a sheet.

In this practice. you will use the Area Analysis tools to create a Gross area plan and a Rentable area plan. You will then add area boundary lines and areas, as shown in Figure 2–29, and modify the area types using an area schedule.

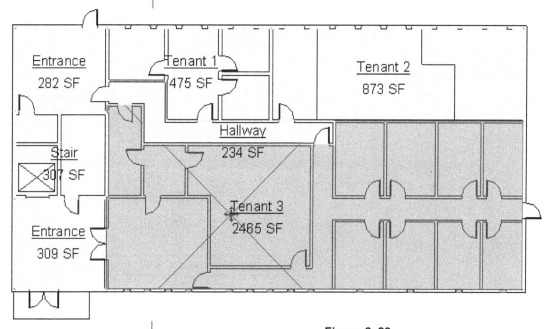

Figure 2–29

- The scale has been changed for clarity.

Task 1 - Create a gross area plan.

1. In the practice files folder, open **Medical-Office-Areas.rvt**.

2. In the *Architecture* tab>Room & Area panel, expand ⊠ (Area) and click ⊡ (Area Plan).

3. In the New Area Plan dialog box, set the *Type* to **Gross Building** and select **Level 1**. Click **OK**.

4. In the alert box, click **Yes**.

5. The gross area plan is created with boundary lines on the outside of the external walls, as shown in Figure 2–30.

    -   To see the area, open the Visibility/Graphic Overrides dialog box, expand *Areas*, and then select **Interior Fill**.

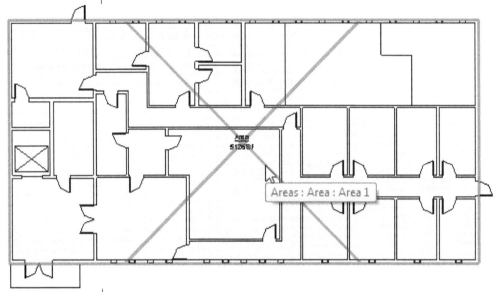

Figure 2–30

6. Save the project.

Task 2 - Create a rentable area plan.

1. In the *Architecture* tab>Room & Area panel, expand (Area) and click (Area Plan).

2. In the New Area Plan dialog box, set the *Type* to **Rentable** and select **Level 1**. Click **OK**.

3. In the alert box, click **Yes** to create boundary lines at external walls. The area boundary is on the inside wall of the building, as shown in Figure 2–31. No areas are created automatically.

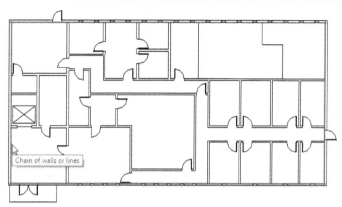

Figure 2–31

4. Open the Visibility/Graphic Overrides dialog box, expand *Areas* and select **Interior Fill**. While you are still in the dialog box, toggle off **Rooms** completely to ensure that you do not select them by mistake.

5. In the *Architecture* tab>Room & Area panel, click ⊠ (Area Boundary). Use ⟋ (Pick Lines) and select the walls shown in Figure 2–32. (Only the new lines are shown.) Modify the lines as required to create closed boundaries.

6. In the *Architecture* tab>Room & Area panel, expand ⊠ (Area) and click ⊠ (Area). Place areas and rename them, as shown in Figure 2–32.

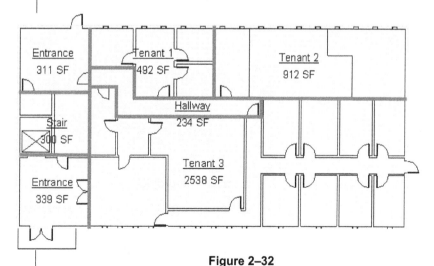

Figure 2–32

7. Save the project.

Task 3 - Change area types using a schedule.

1. Open the **Schedules/Quantities: Area Schedule (Rentable)** view. The areas are listed but all of the *Area Types* are set to the default **Building Common Area**, as shown in Figure 2–33.

<Area Schedule (Rentable)>		
A	B	C
Name	Area Type	Area
Area	Building Common Area	288 SF
Area	Building Common Area	315 SF
Area	Building Common Area	873 SF
Area	Building Common Area	2470 SF
Area	Building Common Area	475 SF
Area	Building Common Area	289 SF

Figure 2–33

2. Change the area types in the schedule, as shown in Figure 2–34. The *Area* values change as the *Area Type* is modified.

<Area Schedule (Rentable)>		
A	B	C
Name	Area Type	Area
Entrance	Building Common Area	282 SF
Entrance	Building Common Area	309 SF
Hallway	Building Common Area	234 SF
Stair	Major Vertical Penetration	307 SF
Tenant 1	Office Area	475 SF
Tenant 2	Office Area	873 SF
Tenant 3	Office Area	2465 SF
	Building Common Area	
	Office Area	
	Exterior Area	
	Floor Area	
	Major Vertical Penetration	
	Store Area	

Figure 2–34

3. Save the project.

4. If you have time, create an additional Rentable area plan for Level 2.

5. Add area boundaries to define several areas on Level 2, and add areas to them.

Task 4 - Add the schedules to a sheet.

1. Create a new sheet file using the default titleblock.

2. Add the area plans and schedule to the sheet, as shown in Figure 2–35.

   - Toggle off the elevation markers in the area plans before you add them to the sheet so that they will fit.

   - Toggle off the area fill (this does not typically need to print).

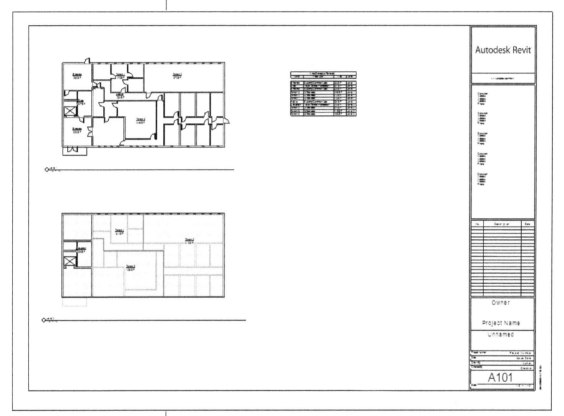

Figure 2–35

2.3 Creating Color Schemes

Color Schemes added to views show information about rooms and areas. For example, if you add data to the room properties, such as Department or Occupancy, you can create a color scheme showing the groups using rooms. If you are using areas, you can identify the area types on an area plan, as shown in Figure 2–36.

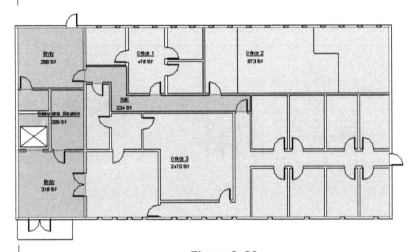

Rentable Area Legend

- Building Common Area
- Office Area

Figure 2–36

How To: Set Up a Color Scheme in a View

1. Create or duplicate a view for the color scheme.

2. In the *Annotate* tab>Color Fill panel, click ⠿ (Color Fill Legend) and place the legend in the view.

3. In the dialog box, select the *Space Type* and *Color Scheme* (as shown in Figure 2–37) and click **OK.** The color scheme is applied to the view, as shown in Figure 2–38.

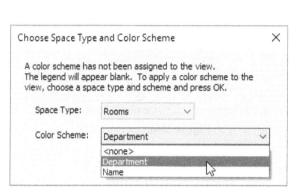

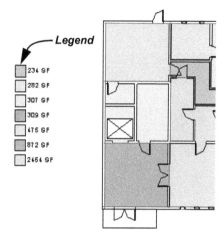

Figure 2–37   Figure 2–38

- You can also select a Color Scheme and place the legend later. In Properties, click the button next to the *Color Scheme*, as shown in Figure 2–39. Then, in the Edit Color Scheme dialog box, in the *Schemes* area, select the *Category* and an existing scheme.

Figure 2–39

- If you change the **Color Scheme** in the View Properties dialog box, it also updates the associated legend.

- You can edit the color scheme through properties or select the **Color Fill Legend** and, in the *Modify | Color Fill Legend*

   tab>Scheme panel, click ⬚✏ (Edit Scheme).

You can set the Color Scheme Location in Properties.

• The color fill of the scheme can display in background or the foreground of the view, as shown in Figure 2–40. This impacts how components display as well as whether or not the color fill stops at the walls.

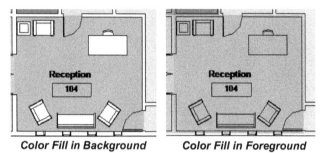

Color Fill in Background   Color Fill in Foreground

Figure 2–40

How To: Define a Color Scheme

1. In View Properties, click the button next to the *Color Scheme* parameter, or in the *Architecture* tab>Room & Area panel, expand the panel title and click 🗒 (Color Schemes).
2. In the Edit Color Scheme dialog box, *Schemes* area, select a *Category*: **Areas (Gross Building)**, **Areas (Rentable)**, or **Rooms**, as shown in Figure 2–41.

Figure 2–41

• Additional options for MEP related elements may also be available, including: Ducts, HVAC Zones, Pipes, and Spaces.

3. Select an existing scheme and click 📋 (Duplicate).
4. In the New color scheme dialog box, enter a new name and click **OK**.
5. In the Edit Color Scheme dialog box, in the *Scheme Definition* area, enter a name for the *Title* of the color scheme. This displays when the legend is placed in the view.

6. In the Color drop-down list, select an option, as shown in Figure 2–42. The available parameters depend on the type of scheme you are creating.

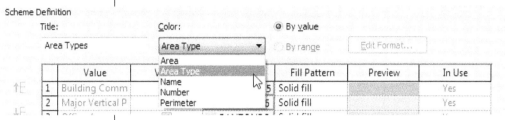

Figure 2–42

7. Select the **By value** or **By range** option to set how the color scheme displays.

8. Click ✛ (Add Value) to add more rows to the scheme, as shown in Figure 2–43. Modify the visibility (*Visible* column), *Color*, and *Fill Pattern* as required.

Figure 2–43

9. In the *Options* area, select **Include elements from linked files** if you are using linked files.
10. Click **OK** to finish.

- Click ↑E (Move Rows Up) or ↓E (Move Rows Down) to change the order of rows in the list.

- To remove a row, select it and click ▭ (Remove Value). This option is only available if the parameter data is not being used in the room or area elements in the project.

Color Schemes By Value

If you select the **By value** option, you can modify the visibility, color, and fill pattern of the scheme. The value is assigned by the parameter data in the room or area object.

- Values are automatically updated when you add data to the parameters used in the color scheme. For example, if you create a color by room *Name* and then add another room name in the project, it is also added to the color scheme.

Color Schemes By Range

If you select the **By range** option, you can modify the *At Least* variable and the *Caption*, as well as the visibility, color, and fill pattern, as shown in Figure 2–44.

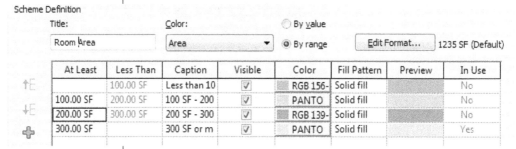

Figure 2–44

- Only the **Area** and **Perimeter** parameters can be set by range.

- Click **Edit Format...** to modify the units display format.

- When you add rows, the new row increments according to the previous distances set or double the value of the first row.

Practice 2c

Create Color Schemes

Practice Objectives

- Apply a color scheme to a view.
- Add a color scheme legend.
- Create **By value** and **By range** color schemes

In this practice, you will add an existing color scheme and a legend to a view, as shown in Figure 2–45. You will also create and apply color schemes By value for Room Names and By range for rentable area sizes.

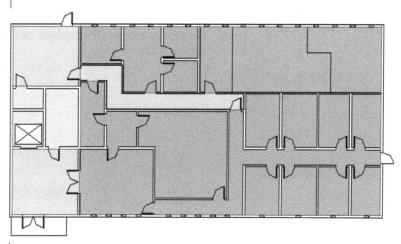

Rentable Area Legend

- Building Common Area
- Major Vertical Penetration
- Office Area

Figure 2–45

Task 1 - Apply a color scheme.

1. In the practice files folder, open **Medical-Office-Colors.rvt**.

2. Duplicate the **Area Plans (Rentable): Level 1** view and name it **Level 1 - Rentable Area**.

3. In the *Annotate tab*>Color Fill panel, click ▦ (Color Fill Legend) and click to the left of the building to place the legend.

4. In the Choose Space Type and Color Scheme dialog boxes, set the *Space Type* to **Areas (Rentable)** and the *Color Scheme* to **Rentable Area**. Click **OK**.

5. The Legend and floor plan are set to the appropriate color fill, as shown in Figure 2–45.

6. Save the project.

Task 2 - Create a Color Scheme

1. Duplicate with detailing the **Area Plans (Rentable)**: **Level 1 - Rentable Area** view and name it **Level 1 - Rentable Area by Size**.

2. Select the legend and in the *Modify | Color Fill Legends* tab> Scheme panel, click (Edit Scheme).

3. Click (Duplicate) to create a copy of the existing area color scheme and name it **Rentable Area by Size**.

4. In the *Scheme Definition* area, enter **Rentable Area by Size** for the *Title* and select **Area** in the Color drop-down list.

5. Select **By range**. The default ranges display, as shown in Figure 2–46.

Any time a warning about colors not being preserved displays, click OK.

Figure 2–46

6. Set the value of the default *At Least* variable to **200 SF**.

7. Click ✛ (Add Value). This should create a value of 400 SF.

8. Select **400 SF** and click ✛ (Add Value) again. Continue working down the menu until you have **1000 SF** in the *At Least* value list, as shown in Figure 2–47.

Figure 2–47

9. Modify any colors or fills as required.

10. Click **OK** to close the dialog box. The new color scheme is applied to the view, as shown in Figure 2–48.

Rentable Area by Size

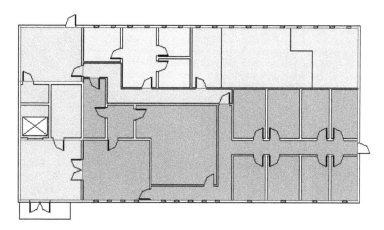

Figure 2–48

11. Save the project.

Task 3 - Create a Room Color Scheme

1. In the *Architecture* tab>Room & Area panel, expand the panel title and select (Color Schemes).

2. In the Edit Color Scheme dialog box, set the *Category* to **Rooms**.

3. Click (Duplicate) to create a copy of the existing room color scheme and name it **Room Names**.

4. In the *Scheme Definition* area, enter **Room Names** for the *Title* and select **Name** in the Color drop-down list.

5. The values are automatically applied according to the room names used in the project, as shown in part in Figure 2–49.

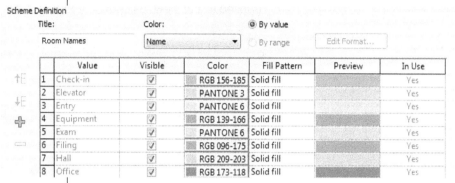

Figure 2–49

6. Click ➕ (Add Value) and create a new value named **Lab**. The new Lab value is set to **No** in the *In Use* column, as shown in Figure 2–50.

Figure 2–50

7. Modify the colors or fill patterns for the scheme as required. (Note that the default black is hard to see in the project.)

8. Click **OK**. The scheme is not applied to the current view when you create it this way.

9. Open the **Floor Plans: Level 1 - Rooms** view.

10. In Properties, select the **Color Scheme** button.

11. In the Edit Color Scheme dialog box, set the *Category* to **Rooms**, select the new **Room Names** color scheme, and click **OK**.

12. In the *Annotate* tab>Color Fill panel, click 🔳 (Color Fill Legend).

13. Place the legend to the side of the building. It automatically displays using the current color scheme, as shown in Figure 2–51.

Room Names

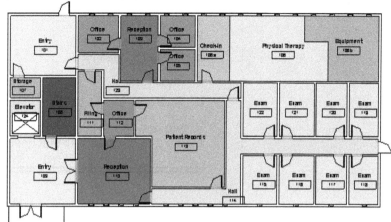

Figure 2–51

14. Change the name of one of the offices to **Lab**. The color updates to match the Lab value you added to the color scheme.

15. Change the name of one of the exam rooms to **Mechanical**. A new value is automatically added to the color scheme, as shown in Figure 2–52.

Room Names

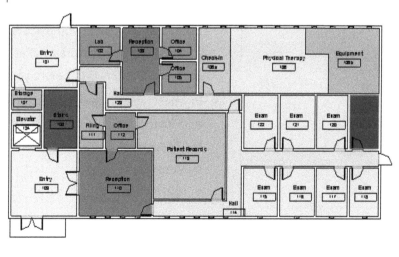

Figure 2–52

16. Save the project.

Chapter Review Questions

1. Which of the following element types can define the boundaries of a room? (Select all that apply.)

   a. Walls

   b. Retaining Walls

   c. Floors

   d. Roofs

2. Where can you set the height of a room, as shown in Figure 2–53? (Select all that apply.)

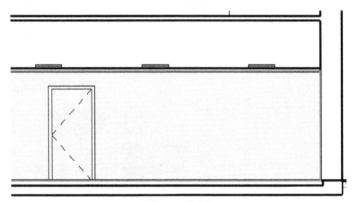

Figure 2–53

   a. In Properties, before or after you place the room.

   b. In a section, after you place the room.

   c. In a floor plan, before or after you place the room.

   d. In the Options Bar, before you place the room.

3. In which type of view do you place areas?

   a. Floor Plans

   b. Sections

   c. Area Plans

   d. Elevations

4. Which of the following need to be in place before you add areas to an area plan, as shown in Figure 2–54?

Figure 2–54

a. Room Boundaries

b. Room Separation Lines

c. Area Separation Lines

d. Area Boundaries

5. If you want to have more than one color scheme that uses the same level and rooms, you need to create a view for each scheme.

a. True

b. False

6. If you are creating a color scheme to display the individual area of each room, as shown in Figure 2–55, which of the following do you use?

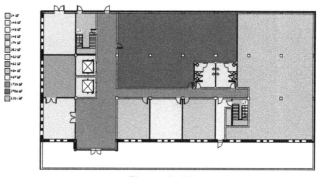

Figure 2–55

a. By Value

b. By Range

Command Summary

Button	Command	Location
	Area	• **Ribbon:** *Architecture* tab>Room & Area panel, expand Area
	Area and Volume Computations	• **Ribbon:** *Architecture* tab>Room & Area panel, expand panel title
	Area Boundary	• **Ribbon:** *Architecture* tab>Room & Area panel
	Area Plan	• **Ribbon:** *Architecture* tab>Room & Area panel, expand Area
	Color Fill Legend	• **Ribbon:** *Annotate* tab>Color Fill panel
	Color Schemes	• **Ribbon:** *Architecture* tab>Room & Area panel, expand panel title
	Room	• **Ribbon:** *Architecture* tab>Room & Area panel • **Shortcut:** RM
	Room Separator	• **Ribbon:** *Architecture* tab>Room & Area panel
	Tag All Not Tagged	• **Ribbon:** *Architecture* tab>Room & Area panel, expand Tag Room or Tag Area
	Tag Area/ Area Tag	• **Ribbon:** *Architecture* tab>Room & Area panel or *Annotate* tab>Tags panel
	Tag Room/ Room Tag	• **Ribbon:** *Architecture* tab>Room & Area panel or *Annotate* tab>Tags panel • **Shortcut:** RT

Chapter 3

Visualization

For the architectural community, one of the most powerful features of Autodesk® Revit® is the ability to create views that enable you to display the building design in its full, 3D expression. Not only can you create perspective views, but you can also make any 2D or 3D view look like it was hand-sketched or realistic. You can create exploded orthographic views - each of which can help others understand your design. You can also visually test the design using sun studies that show exactly how sun and shadows would impact the building.

Learning Objectives in this Chapter

- Create perspective views using the Camera tool.
- Modify a view using Graphics Display Options such as Sketchy Lines and Depth Cueing.
- Displace elements in a view to create an exploded view.
- Set True North and the project location to prepare a project for solar studies.
- Graphically display sun locations and its impact on the project using the Sun Path with shadows.
- Create solar studies, including still, single-day, and multi-day studies.

3.1 Creating Perspective Views

Perspectives, as shown in Figure 3–1, provide more realistic views of buildings that can help designers visualize and pass on information to others who might not understand plans and elevations. They are easily created using the **Camera** command by specifying a camera location and a target.

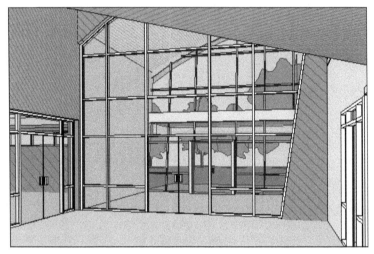

Figure 3–1

- You can add, delete, modify, and move elements in 3D perspective views.

- Perspective views can be placed on sheets.

How To: Create a Perspective

1. Open a plan view.
2. In the Quick Access Toolbar (or the *View* tab>Create panel),
   expand 🏠 (3D View) and click 📷 (Camera).
3. In the Options Bar, select **Perspective** and set an *Offset* for the camera *From* one of the levels, as shown in Figure 3–2. This is the height of the camera.
   - To create orthographic views, clear the **Perspective** option and select a scale for the view.

Figure 3–2

4. Select a point on the drawing to place the camera.
5. Select another point for the target location, as shown in Figure 3–3.

To create an interior perspective, place the camera inside the room.

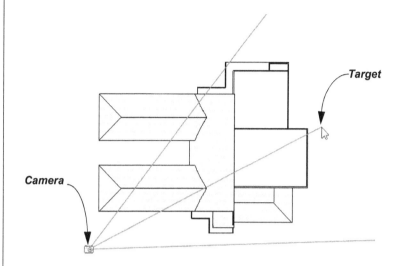

Figure 3–3

6. A new 3D view is created and opened as shown in Figure 3–4.

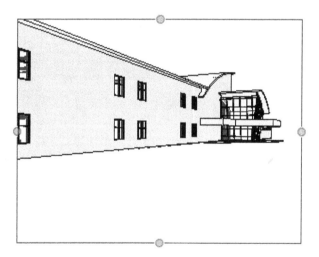

Figure 3–4

7. In the Project Browser, right-click on the new 3D view and rename it, as required.

• If you do not want the 3D View to be cropped, in the View Control Bar, click ⊞ (Do Not Crop View).

Modifying Perspectives

Perspectives can be modified by changing the camera information using controls or the camera properties. You can also modify the view size through a dialog box.

- Use the ViewCube or the mouse (<Shift>+ middle mouse button) to rotate the view.

- You can switch between Perspective and Isometric mode by right-clicking on the View Cube and selecting **Perspective** or **Orthographic**. You can also change this in the view properties.

- To change the field of view, select the shape handles of the crop region and manipulate them so that they show the required part of the building, as shown in Figure 3–5.

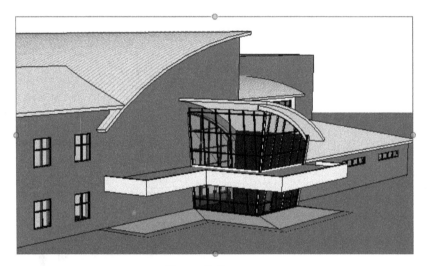

Figure 3–5

- To toggle off the box around the perspective, in Properties, clear the **Crop Region Visible** option or in the View Control Bar, click ⚐ *(Hide Crop Region)*.

- *Change the Visual Style* to **Shaded, Consistent Colors**, or **Realistic** to see a representation of the materials.

How To: Modify the Camera

1. Open the 3D camera view and one other view and tile them.
2. Select the edge of the camera view crop region and the camera displays in the other view.
    - Another way to make a camera display in a plan view: right-click on the perspective view in the Project Browser and select **Show Camera**.

3. Drag the controls for the camera, target, and far clip plane, as shown in Figure 3–6, to new locations.

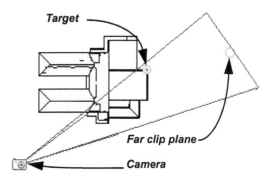

Figure 3–6

* The target is what the eye sees. The far clip plane needs to be located beyond the information you want to see in the view.

* You can make changes to cameras in Properties by scrolling down to the *Extents* and *Camera* sections, as shown in Figure 3–7.

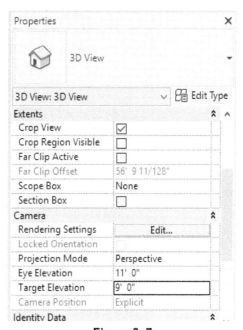

Figure 3–7

* For a true 2-point perspective, ensure that both the *Target Elevation* and *Eye Elevation* are the same height.

How To: Modify View Size

1. In the *Modify | Cameras* tab>Crop panel, click  (Size Crop).
2. In the Crop Region Size dialog box (shown in Figure 3–8), specify an exact *Width* and *Height* for the view.

Crop Region Size	✕
Model Crop Size	
Width:	Height:
3ʺ	4 1/2ʺ
Change	
◉ Field of view	
○ Scale (locked proportions)	
OK Cancel Apply Help	

Figure 3–8

- Select **Field of view** to resize both the *Height* and *Width* of the crop region.
- Select **Scale (locked proportions)** to lock the proportions of the crop region. When you change the width, the height adjusts proportionally.

Hint: Surface Transparency Sliders

While creating a perspective view, you are sometimes required to see behind a wall. You can toggle off an individual wall using **Hide in View>Elements**, or make the wall transparent as shown Figure 3–9.

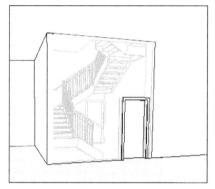

Figure 3–9

How To: Adjust Transparency

1. Select the element(s), right-click, and select **Override Graphics in View>By Element...**
2. In the dialog box, expand the *Surface Transparency* area and adjust the slider bar as required, as shown in Figure 3–10.

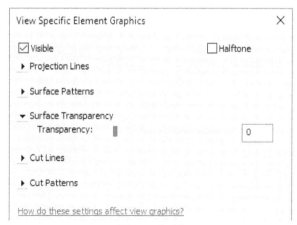

Figure 3–10

- Surface patterns (such as brick) are not affected by the transparency setting; so, you may want to toggle them off in the *Surface Patterns* area, when working with transparency.

Practice 3a | Create Perspective Views

Practice Objective

- Create exterior and interior perspective views.

In this practice, you will create an interior perspective and an exterior perspective, as shown in Figure 3–11.

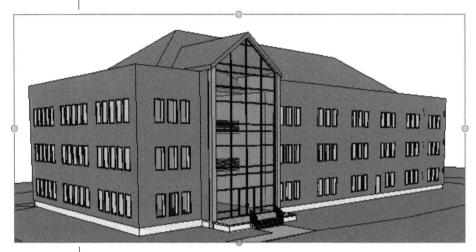

Figure 3–11

Task 1 - Create an Exterior Perspective View.

1. In the practice files folder, open **Midrise-Perspective.rvt**.

2. Open the **Floor Plans: Level 1** view.

3. In the *View* tab>Create panel, expand 🏠 (3D View) and click 📷 (Camera).

4. Create an exterior perspective named **Front Perspective**, showing the front of the building and set the *Visual Style* to **Consistant Colors**, as shown in Figure 3–11.

5. Modify the camera properties as required, to get a good view. Hold <Shift>+middle mouse button to rotate the view.

Task 2 - Create an Interior Perspective View.

1. Repeat the command and create an interior perspective named **Office Perspective**, as shown in Figure 3–12.

If the corner of the room does not display, change the far clip view.

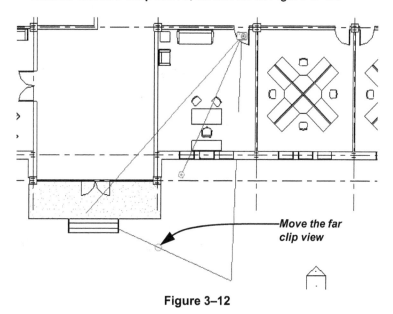

Move the far clip view

Figure 3–12

2. Save the project.

3.2 Working with Graphic Display Options

Even without creating a rendering, you can set up striking views using graphics display options. These include tools for setting up the model display of surfaces and edges, shadows, sketchy lines for preliminary views, and added depth cueing for automatic lineweight control, and backgrounds as shown in Figure 3–13.

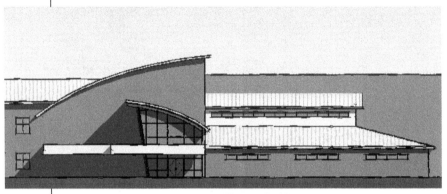

Figure 3–13

Additionally, you can enter GD.

- In the View Control Bar, expand the **Visual Style** icon and select **Graphic Display Options...**, as shown in Figure 3–14.

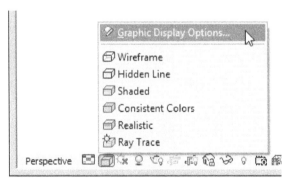

Figure 3–14

- The dialog box displays, as shown in Figure 3–15.

Figure 3–15

- The settings that are selected in the Graphic Display Options dialog box can be saved as a View Template.

Model Display

In the Graphic Display Options dialog box, in the *Model Display* area, you can set the visual *Style*, *Transparency* (for all objects in the view), and select a linetype from the *Silhouettes* drop-down list. This override enables you to specify the type of lines used to outline various parts of a building in a view, as shown in Figure 3–16.

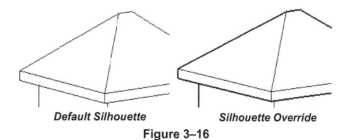

Default Silhouette   *Silhouette Override*

Figure 3–16

Hint: Adjusting Linework

To emphasize a particular line or change the look of a line in elevations and other views, modify the lines using the **Linework** command. These changes are view-specific, applying only to the view in which you make them, as shown in Figure 3–17.

Figure 3–17

- The **Linework** command can be used on project edges and cut edges of model elements, edges in imported CAD files, and edges in linked Autodesk Revit models.

How To: Adjust Linework

1. In the *Modify* tab>View panel, click ⟱ (Linework) or enter the shortcut **LW**.
2. In the *Modify | Linework* tab>Line Style panel, select the line style you want to use from the list.
3. Move the cursor and highlight the line you want to change. Use <Tab> to toggle through the lines as required.
4. Click on the line to change it to the new line style.
5. Click on other lines as required, or return to the **Modify** command to finish.

If the line is too long or short, you can modify the length using the controls at the end of the line.

- The **Linework** tool overrides any other graphic changes to the view.

Shadows

In the Graphic Display Options dialog box, in the *Shadows* area, select **Cast Shadows**, as shown Figure 3–18. You can also select **Show Ambient Shadows**. Ambient shadows look more realistic as shadows are added to corners and other dark areas, but they make the view much darker.

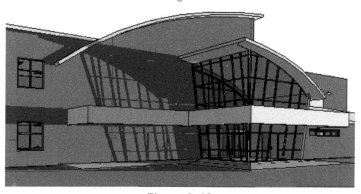

Figure 3–18

Sketchy Lines

Autodesk Revit models can look polished even at the conceptual stage. Some people prefer to show clients a presentation that looks like it is hand-drawn. To do this, you can set up a view using sketchy lines, as shown in Figure 3–19.

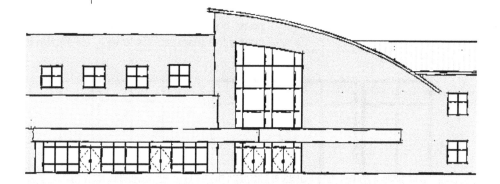

Figure 3–19

- Sketchy lines can be used in all types of views, including: plans, elevations, sections, 3D orthographic, and perspective views.

- Datums (levels and grids) and annotation items are not impacted by sketchy lines.

- Views using sketchy lines can be exported to an image file, printed, and put on sheets.

How To: Modify a View Using Sketchy Lines

1. Set up a view where you want to apply a hand-drawn look.
2. In the View Control Bar, click on the **Visual Style** button and select **Graphic Display Options**. Alternatively, in Properties, beside the **Graphic Display Options...**, click **Edit...**.
3. In the Graphic Display Options dialog box, expand the *Sketchy Lines* area.
4. Select **Enable Sketchy Lines** and move the sliders for *Jitter* and *Extension*, as shown in Figure 3–20.

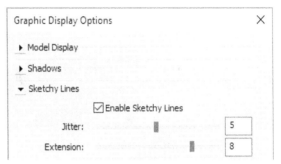

Figure 3–20

- *Jitter* controls how wavy the lines are and how many layers of lines there are. It varies from 0, where the lines are perfectly straight, to 10, which has multiple layers of wavy lines, as shown in Figure 3–21.

- *Extension* controls the length of the line beyond the end point. It varies from 0, where there is no extension, to 10 where the extension is longer, as shown in Figure 3–22.

Figure 3–21

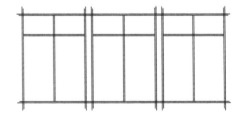

Figure 3–22

5. Click **Apply** to see the change to the view.
6. When you are satisfied with the look, click **OK**.

Depth Cueing

Another important visual aid, called depth cueing, gives you a sense of depth by fading elements in the distance, as shown in Figure 3–23. This is set up in the Graphic Display Options dialog box.

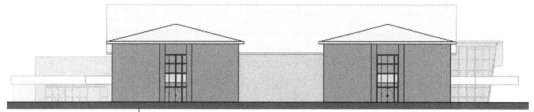

Figure 3–23

- Depth cueing is specifically used for elevations and sections and does not work in plan or 3D views.

- The *Far Clipping* and *Far Clip Offset* parameters, which are set up in Properties (as shown in Figure 3–24), impact how depth cueing works. In the Far Clipping dialog box, select one of the clip methods, as shown in Figure 3–25 and click **OK**. Then, set a useful *Far Clip Offset* for the building.

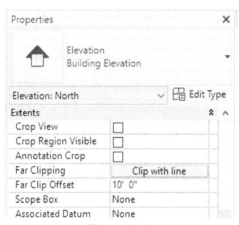

Figure 3–24

Figure 3–25

- You can try changing the *Far Clip Offset* before adjusting the view in the Graphics Display Options dialog box, as depth cueing is based on the location of the front and back view clip planes.

How To: Establish a sense of depth in a view

1. Set up a view where you want to apply depth cueing
2. In Properties, set up a *Far Clipping* method and a *Far Clip Offset*.
3. Open the Graphic Display Options dialog box and expand *Depth Cueing*.
4. Select **Show Depth** and click **Apply** to see how the default settings work.
5. Move the sliders for *Fade Start/End Location* and *Fade Limit (%)* as required, as shown in Figure 3–26.

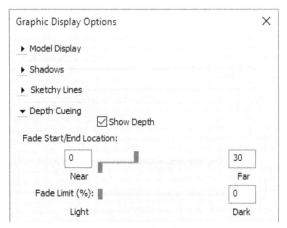

Figure 3–26

- *Fade Start/End Location* controls the start and end of the fading. *Near* and *Far* are the percentage away from the front and back view clip planes.

- The *Fade Limit (%)* intensity can be set from *Light* to *Dark*.

6. Click **Apply** to see the change to the view.
7. When you are satisfied with the look, click **OK**.

Background

In the *Background* area, in the Background drop-down list, select one of the following four options: **None**, **Sky**, which give a default sky appearance and enables you to specify a ground color, **Gradient** (shown in Figure 3–27 and Figure 3–28), or **Image**, which enables you to select a custom background image

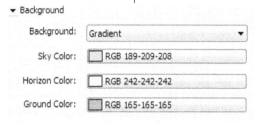

Figure 3–27

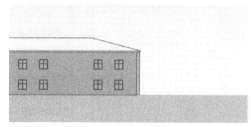

Figure 3–28

Lighting and Photographic Exposure

When you are in the **Realistic** or **Ray Trace** visual style, in the *Lighting* area (shown in Figure 3–29), you can set the *Sun Settings* and specify the intensity of the *Sun*, *Ambient Light*, and *Shadows*. You can also specify *Artificial Lights* if you have lighting fixtures in the project and want to specify which ones will be used in the view.

The concepts in the Lighting and Photographic Exposure areas are covered in more depth in Sun Studies and Rendering.

Figure 3–29

In the *Photographic Exposure* area (shown in Figure 3–30), you can modify the artificial lights to set the best exposure to a scene.

Figure 3–30

Practice 3b

Work with Graphic Display Options

Practice Objectives

- Use Sketchy Lines and other Graphic Display Options.
- Set up a 3D view oriented to a 2D view.
- Investigate Depth Cueing.

In this practice, you will set up an elevation view of the front entrance and modify the look using sketchy lines. You will then duplicate the view and set it up to look more realistic as shown in Figure 3–31 You will also create a 3D elevation view and modify another view using Depth Cueing and how the Far Clip plane and offset impacts the view.

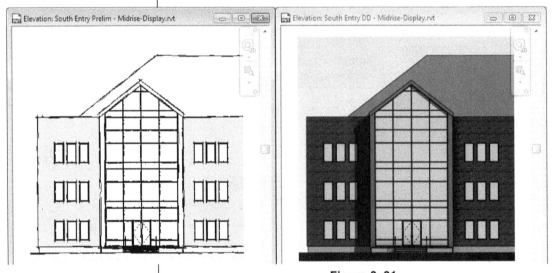

Figure 3–31

Task 1 - Set up a view using Sketchy Lines.

1. In the practice files folder, open **Midrise-Display.rvt**.

2. In the Project Browser, duplicate the **Elevations (Building Elevation): South** view and rename it to **South Entry Prelim**.

3. Hide the level lines. (Select a level and enter **VH** to hide the category.)

4. In the View Control Bar, click 🔲 (Show Crop Region).

5. Modify the crop region so you are only seeing the entry area of the building, as shown in Figure 3–32.

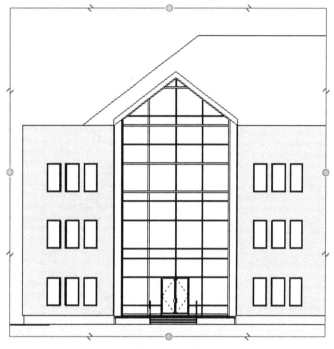

Figure 3–32

6. In the View Control Bar, click 🔲 (Hide Crop Region).

7. In Properties, beside Graphic Display Options, click **Edit...**.

8. In the Graphic Display Options dialog box, expand the Sketchy Lines area and select **Enable Sketchy Lines.**

9. Move the dialog box over to the side so you can see the view, if required.

10. Slide the *Jitter* bar to around **5** and click **Apply**. The lines take on a sketch-like look, as shown in Figure 3–33.

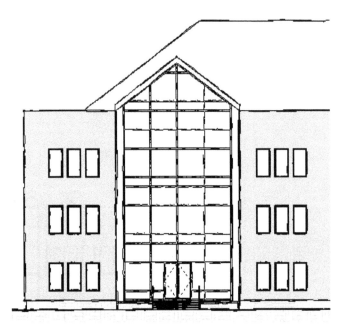

Figure 3–33

11. Try several different looks by manipulating the *Jitter* and *Extension* slider bars. Click **Apply** after each change to see the variations.

12. Click **OK** when you have the required look.

13. Save the project.

Task 2 - Set up a view using Shadows and the Realistic visual style.

---

1. Duplicate the **South Entry Prelim** view and name it **South Entry DD**.

2. Open the Graphic Display Options dialog box. (**Hint:** Enter **GD**).

3. Toggle off **Sketchy Lines** and click **OK**.

4. In the View Control Bar, click ⌖ (Shadows Off) to toggle shadows on.

There are several image files you can use in the practice files folder.

5. Try out the various visual styles to see how they look with the view. End on the **Realistic** visual style.

6. Open the Graphic Display Options dialog box.

7. In the *Model Display* area, select **Smooth lines with anti-aliasing** and click **Apply** to see the changes.

8. Expand *Shadows*, select **Show Ambient Shadows**, and click **Apply** to see the changes.

9. Expand *Background* and test out several different options. Click **OK** and the background is applied, such as the gradient shown in Figure 3–34.

Figure 3–34

10. Close all other views except the **South Entry Prelim** and **South Entry DD** views.

11. Enter **WT** to tile them and then **ZA** to zoom so they fit in each window.

12. Save the project.

Task 3 - Create a 3D Elevation view

1. Open the default 3D view.

2. Rename it **South Entry**.

3. Right-click on the ViewCube and select **Orient to View> Elevations>Elevation: South Entry DD**, as shown in Figure 3–35.

You can move around the view in Interactive Ray Trace Mode.

4. Test out several different Visual Styles with this view. The glass is transparent and you can see into the building. You can also apply the **Ray Trace** visual style, as shown in Figure 3–36.

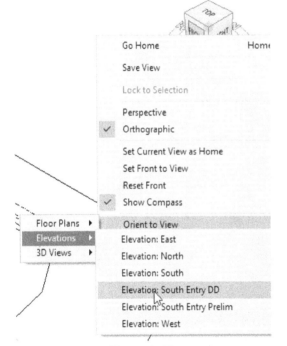

Figure 3–35

Figure 3–36

5. While still in the Interactive Ray Trace Mode, in Properties, note that you cannot modify *Graphic Display Options*.

6. In the View Control Bar, expand 🏠 (Ray Trace) and select **Graphic Display Options...**

7. The dialog box opens with *Lighting*, *Photographic Exposure*, and *Background* expanded. You cannot make changes to the other options.

8. Close the dialog box.

9. Save the project.

Task 4 - Apply Depth Cueing to a view.

1. Open the **Elevations: South** view.

2. Set the *Visual Style* to **Shaded**.

3. Open the Graphic Display Options dialog box and toggle on **Show Depth**, but do not make any changes yet. Click **OK**.

4. In Properties, set *Far Clipping* to **Clip with line**. By default, the *Far Clip Offset* is set to **10'-0"**. This distance is not deep enough to show the building so only the toposurface displays as shown in Figure 3–37.

Figure 3–37

5. Test several *Far Clip Offset* distances in increments of 10 (e.g. 20', 30', 40') and finish with **100'-0"**. The building displays with a shaded roof, as shown in Figure 3–38.

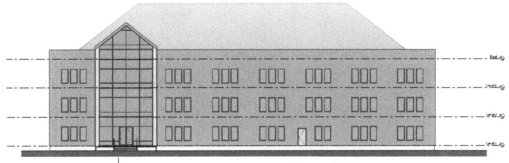

Figure 3–38

6. Open the Graphic Display Options dialog box and make any required changes to the *Depth Cueing* options.

7. Save the project.

3.3 Adding Exploded Views

You can use displacement sets to create exploded views that can be used to explain a project or detail a complex detail. These views update as you work on a project, any other view does. They can be created in 3D perspective or orthographic views, such as that shown in Figure 3–39.

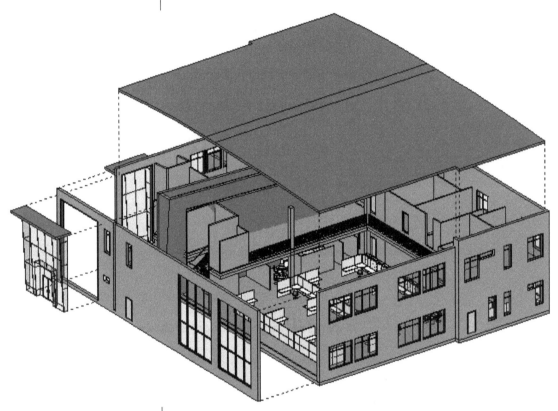

Figure 3–39

• Displaced views are full 3D views and can be rotated using the mouse or ViewCube.

How To: Displace Elements

1. Select the element or elements that you want to displace.
2. In the *Modify | <element type>* tab>View panel, click

   🖼️ (Displace Elements).
3. In Properties, set the *X*, *Y*, and/or *Z Displacement* or use the drag controls on the face of the element, as shown in Figure 3–40.

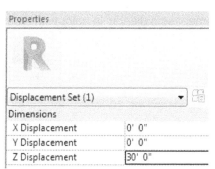
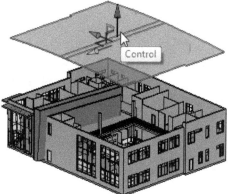

Figure 3–40

4. To display projection lines from the original location to the displacement, in the *Modify | Displacement Set* tab>

   Displacement Set panel, click ✎ (Path).
5. Select the corner of the displaced element where you want to locate the path.

- When displacing a wall, elements (such as doors and windows) are also displaced. You can displace them separately by using <Tab> to select them once you have displaced the wall.

- Storefront curtain wall elements are not displaced with the walls in which they are located. You can add them to the displacement set or displace them separately.

- If you want to displace a door or window separately from a wall, press <Tab> until the element is highlighted and then follow the steps for displacing elements.

- If you no longer want an element to be displaced, select it, and in the *Modify | Displacement Set* tab>Displacement Set panel, click 🗇 (Reset).

- To display the displacements sets in a view, in the View Control Bar, click 🗇 (Highlight Displacement Sets). The displacement sets display in color with a rim around the edge of the view, as shown in Figure 3–41.

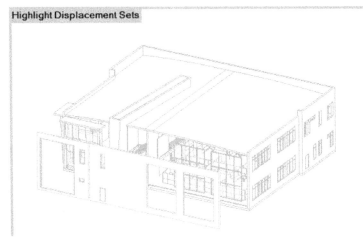

Figure 3–41

How To: Edit Displaced Elements

1. Select a displaced element.
2. In the *Modify | Displacement Set* tab>Displacement Set panel, click 🗇 (Edit). The existing displacement set is highlighted.

3. Verify that 🔲 (Add) is selected in the floating Edit Displacement Set panel and select the elements you want to include in the displacement set, as shown in Figure 3–42.

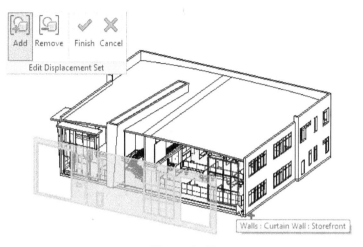

Figure 3–42

4. As you select the elements, they are moved into place and highlighted.
5. If you do not want an element to be in the displacement set, click 🔲 (Remove) and select the element. The element returns to place.

6. Click ✓ (Finish).

• It is sometimes easier to displace one element (such as a wall) and then add other elements to the set.

Practice 3c

Add Exploded Views

Practice Objectives

- Displace elements in a view to create an exploded view.
- Add elements to a displacement set.

In this practice, you will create a 3D view in which you will set up several displacement sets to create an exploded view of the building. You will also add an element to a set and place paths that display the location. An example of a finished view is shown in Figure 3–43 with the displacement sets highlighted.

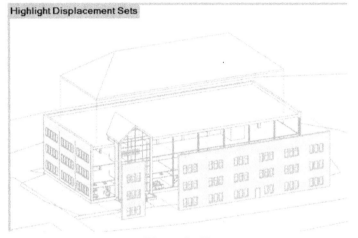

Figure 3–43

Task 1 - Create displacement sets.

1. In the practice files folder, open **Midrise-Exploded.rvt**.

2. Open the **3D Views: 3D-Exploded** view.

3. Rotate the view so it is similar in orientation to that shown in Figure 3–43.

4. Select the brick wall on the front left.

5. In the *Modify | Walls* tab>View panel, click ☂ (Displace Elements).

In this case, you need to move the control in the direction opposite to the arrow.

6. Use the control to drag it away from the building, as shown in Figure 3–44.

Figure 3–44

7. Select the hipped roof, click 📬 (Displace Elements), and move it up using the control or Properties.

8. Select the first wall that you displaced. In the *Modify | Displacement Set* tab>Displacement Set panel, click 📇 (Edit).

9. In the Edit Displacement Set floating panel, ensure that 🔲 (Add) is selected and click on the longer front brick wall. It moves to match the location, as shown in Figure 3–45.

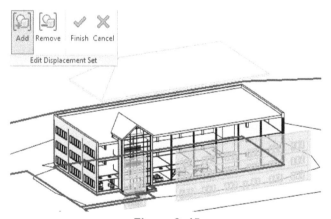

Figure 3–45

10. Click ✔ (Finish).

11. With the elements still selected, click ✐ (Path).

12. Select the corners of each wall and the corners of the roof to place the lines.

13. Displace other elements of the building, as required.

14. Save the project.

3.4 Setting Up Solar Studies

The next step in enhancing your views is to get the sun in the correct place so that you can see how shadows impact your project. First, you need to establish the geographical location of the project and the true north direction. Then, you can graphically set year and time of day using the sun path, as shown in Figure 3–46. From there, you can create still, single day, and multi-day solar studies that show more accurate time settings.

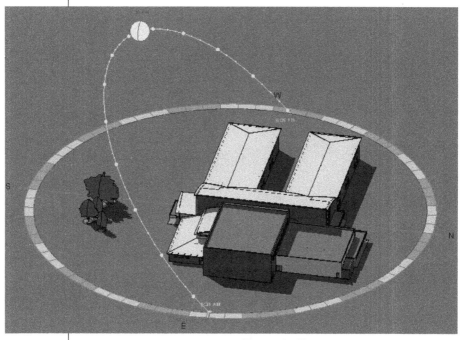

Figure 3–46

In the View Control Bar, toggle on **Sun Path** and **Shadows**, as shown in Figure 3–47.

Toggle shadows off when you do not need them to conserve memory resources.

Figure 3–47

- The sun path and shadows can be used in 2D and 3D views.

Preparing for Solar Studies

The geographic location of a project and the true north orientation of the model on the site impact solar studies. Most buildings are modeled with north at the top of the primary axis, as shown in Figure 3–48. True north can be set in a site plan view, as shown in Figure 3–49.

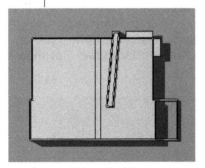

Figure 3–48

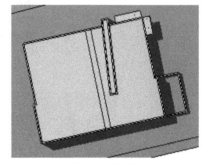

Figure 3–49

- If you are working with a linked DWG file, you can use the geographic data stored in that file.

How To: Set True North

1. Duplicate the **Floor Plans: Site** view and rename it **Site - True North**.
2. In Properties, set the *Orientation* to **True North**, as shown in Figure 3–50.

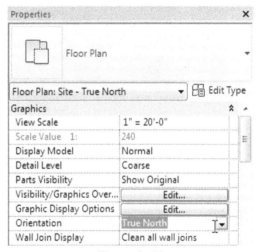

Figure 3–50

3. In the *Manage* tab>Project Location panel, expand (Position) and click (Rotate True North).

4. In the Options Bar, enter a value for *Angle from Project to True North,* or select two points on the screen to define the angle (similar to the **Rotate** command). The entire project rotates, as shown in Figure 3–51.

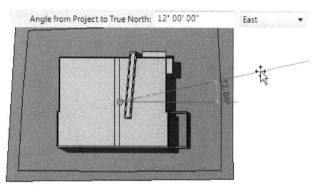

Figure 3–51

How To: Manage the Location for a Project

1. In the *Manage* tab>Project Location panel, click
   (Location).

2. In the Location Weather and Site dialog box>*Location* tab, you can set the *Define Location by*: the **Default City List** (typically used for HVAC sizing), as shown in Figure 3–52, or **Internet Mapping Service** (typically used for energy analysis), as shown in Figure 3–53.

Figure 3–52

Figure 3–53

Using the Sun Path

If you want to graphically set the sun locations, you can use the sun path to specify the date and time of day by dragging the sun icon around the path or analemma, as shown in Figure 3–54.

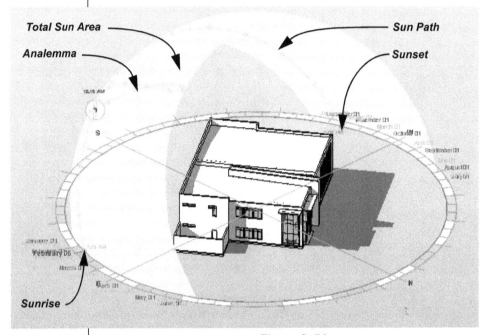

Figure 3–54

How To: Use the Sun Path

1. In the View Control Bar, expand 🔆 (Sun Path Off) and click 🔅 (Sun Path On).
   - If you have not already applied the appropriate sun settings, an alert box displays. Select **Use the specified project location, date, and time instead** to apply the default settings. The other option will not display the sun.
2. Move the sun along the path to change the time of day.
3. Move the sun along the analemma to retain the time of day but change the month.

4. Click on the time of day or the month and change the number, as shown in Figure 3–55.

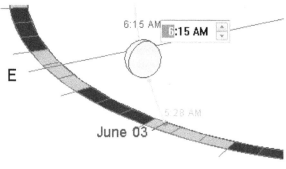

Figure 3–55

Creating Solar Studies

To create solar studies you will use the Sun Settings dialog box, where you can set up the information for still, single day, and multi-day options. Additionally, you can use several preset studies.

• Shadows need to be on to display the solar studies.

How To: Create Solar Studies

At least one solar study is always available.

1. In the View Control Bar, expand the Sun Path drop-down list and click **Sun Settings**, as shown in Figure 3–56. You can also access the Sun Settings in Properties, through the Graphic Display Options dialog box.

Figure 3–56

2. In the Sun Settings dialog box, *Solar Study* area, select the type of study you want to create: **Still**, **Single Day**, or **Multi-Day**.
3. In the *Presets* area, select an existing study and click

   🗋 (Duplicate).
4. In the Name dialog box, enter a name for the study and click **OK**.

- For **Still** studies, in the *Settings* area, specify the *Location*, *Date*, and *Time*, as shown in Figure 3–57.

Figure 3–57

*The **Sunrise to sunset** option automatically calculate the times based on the date.*

- For **Single Day** studies, in the *Settings* area, (shown in Figure 3–58) specify the *Location*, *Date*, and *Time* (start and end). Select the *Time Interval* (**15**, **30**, **45 minutes** or **1 hour**). The *Frames* value is read-only.

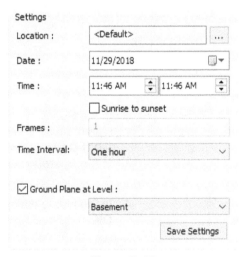

Figure 3–58

- For **Multi-Day** studies, in the *Settings* area, specify the *Date* range, and the *Time* and the *Time Interval*, which is typically set to **One day** or more, as shown in Figure 3–59.

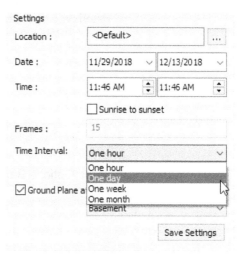

Figure 3–59

5. Click **OK** to close the dialog box and apply the still solar study to the view.

Hint: Setting the Ground Plane

In each type of solar study, you can set the **Ground Plane at Level**, as shown on the left in Figure 3–60, or leave this option cleared. If you do not have site information in the drawing or you are working with an interior view, specify a level. If you have site information (topography) in the drawing, do not specify a level for the ground plane so that the shadows flow over the contours, as shown on the right in Figure 3–60.

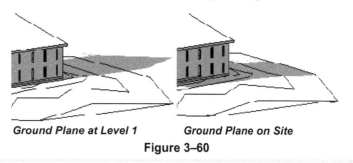

Ground Plane at Level 1   *Ground Plane on Site*

Figure 3–60

How To: View Solar Studies

1. Toggle on shadows.

2. In the View Control Bar, click ☼ (Sun Path Off) and select **Preview Solar Study**, as shown in Figure 3–61.

Figure 3–61

3. In the Options Bar (shown in Figure 3–62), specify the frame at which you want to start and click ▶ (Play).

Figure 3–62

How To: Export Solar Studies

1. Toggle on shadows and ensure that you are in either a **Single-Day** or **Multi-Day** solar study type.

2. In the *File* tab, expand ⬚ (Export)> ⬚ (Images and Animations), and then click ⬚ (Solar Study).

3. In the Length/Format dialog box, specify the *Output Length* and *Format*, as shown in Figure 3–63.

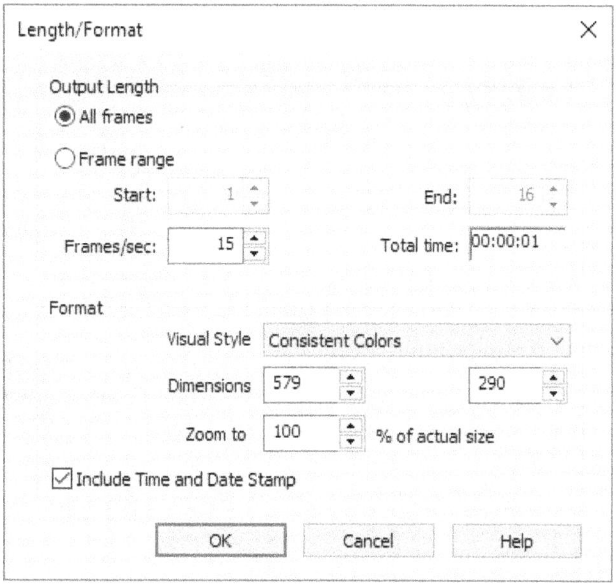

Length/Format   ✕

Output Length
◉ All frames

◯ Frame range
Start: 1   End: 16

Frames/sec: 15   Total time: 00:00:01

Format
Visual Style   Consistent Colors   ⌄

Dimensions   579   290

Zoom to   100   % of actual size

☑ Include Time and Date Stamp

OK   Cancel   Help

Figure 3–63

4. Click **OK**.
5. In the Export Animated Solar Study dialog box, navigate to a folder and specify a file name.

   • By default, the file name is the name of the project plus the name of the Solar Study.

6. Specify the file format, as shown in Figure 3–64, and click **Save**.

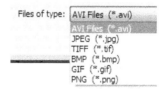

Figure 3–64

7. In the Video Compression dialog box, select the type of *Compression*, as shown in Figure 3–65, and specify any other options. Click **OK**.

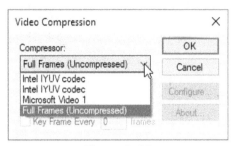

Figure 3–65

- The new animation is processed and can be viewed using the related video software.

Practice 3d

Set up Solar Studies

Practice Objectives

- Set the True North and establish the project location to prepare a project for solar studies.
- Create a Still Solar Study, a Single-Day Solar Study, and a Multi-Day Solar Study.

In this practice, you will create solar studies for your location using the three methods: **Still**, as shown in Figure 3–66, **Single-Day**, and **Multi-Day**.

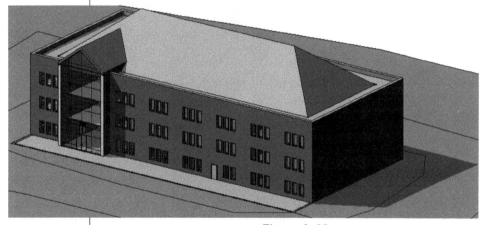

Figure 3–66

Task 1 - Prepare the Project for Solar Studies.

1. In the practice files folder, open **Midrise-Solar.rvt**.

2. Duplicate a copy of the **Floor Plans: Site** view and rename it **Site-True North**. Open the new view.

3. In Properties, set the *Orientation* to **True North**.

4. In the *Manage* tab>Project Location panel, expand (Position) and click (Rotate True North).

5. In the Options Bar, set the *Angle from Project to True North* to **23°** from **East** and press <Enter> for it to take effect. The site plan rotates, as shown in Figure 3–67.

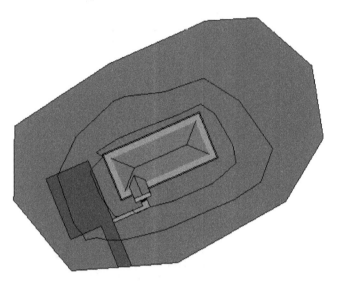

Figure 3–67

6. In the *Manage* tab>Project Location panel, click

   (Location).

7. In the *Location* tab, select your city, or one close to you, in the **Default City List** or from the **Internet Mapping Service** map. Select **Use Daylight Savings Time**, if this applies. Click **OK**.

Task 2 - Create a Still Solar Study.

---

1. Create a new default 3D view that shows the front of the building and the site. Rename the view to **Still Solar Study**.

2. In the View Control Bar, set the *Model Graphics Style* to (Consistant Colors) and enable (Shadows On).

3. In the View Control Bar, enable (Sun Path On). When the Sun Path - Sun Not Displayed dialog box opens, select **Use the specified project location, date and time instead**.

4. Expand (Sun Path On) and select **Sun Settings...**

5. In the Sun Settings dialog box, S*olar Study* area, select **Still**.

You can also set up these options in the Graphic Display Options dialog box.

6. In the *Settings* area, specify today's date and time. To easily get to today's date, expand and click **Today**, as shown in Figure 3–68.

Figure 3–68

7. Click **OK** to close the dialog box. The solar study displays according to your location and time, similar to that shown in Figure 3–69.

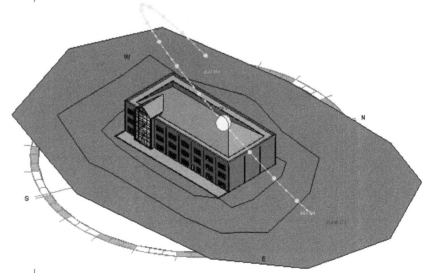

Figure 3–69

8. Use the graphic tools to select another day and time.

9. Save the project.

Task 3 - Create a Single-Day Solar Study.

1. Duplicate the **Still Solar Study** view.

2. Rename the new view to **Single-Day Solar Study**.

3. Toggle off the sun path.

4. Open the Sun Settings dialog box and create a new Single Day solar study - for today's date, from sunrise to sunset, with a *Time Interval* of **15 minutes**.

5. Click **OK** to close the dialog box.

6. In the View Control Bar, click 🔆 (Sun Path Off) and select **Preview Solar Study**. (If this is not available, verify that the shadows are on.)

7. In the Options Bar, click ▶ (Play). The shadows move across the building, as shown for one frame in Figure 3–70.

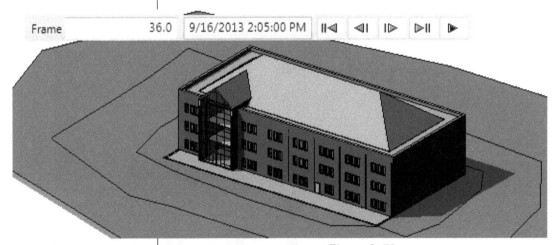

| Frame | | 36.0 | 9/16/2013 2:05:00 PM | ◁ | ◁ | ▷ | ▷ | ▶ |

Figure 3–70

Task 4 - Create a Multi-Day Solar Study.

1. Duplicate the **Single-Day Solar Study** view.

2. Rename the new view as **Multi-Day Solar Study**.

3. Open the Sun Settings dialog box and create a new Multi-Day solar study, for one year at noon with a *Time Interval* of **One month**.

4. Click **OK** and preview the solar study animation.

5. Use ▷ (Next Frame) and step through each month.

6. In what month does the least sun reach into the front entrance of the building, as shown in Figure 3–71?

Your view might vary depending on the location of your building.

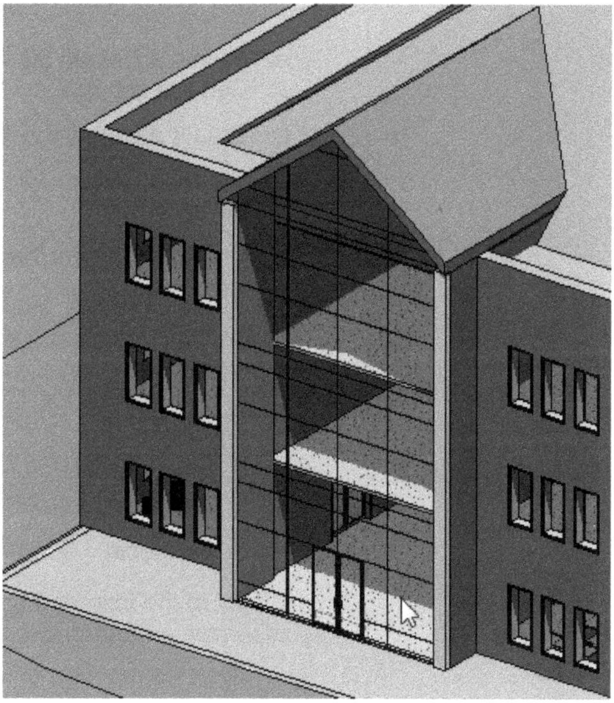

Figure 3–71

7. Save the drawing.

Chapter Review Questions

1. How do you create a perspective view, as shown in Figure 3–72?

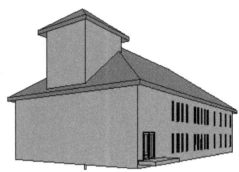

Figure 3–72

   a. Create a Default 3D view and, in Properties, modify the Camera settings.

   b. Create a Camera view.

   c. Create a Default 3D view and, in Properties, select **Perspective**.

   d. Create a Camera view and, in Properties, select **Perspective**.

2. Where can you set the Eye and Target Elevations of a camera?

   a. In Properties.

   b. In the Options Bar.

   c. In the View Control Bar.

   d. In the *Modify | Camera* tab in the ribbon.

3. Which of the following types of views can you customize to resemble a hand-drawn sketch? (Select all that apply.)

   a. Floor Plans

   b. Perspectives

   c. 3D Orthographic Views

   d. Elevations

4. When creating an exploded view, how do you add the dashed lines that connect to the origins, as shown in Figure 3–73?

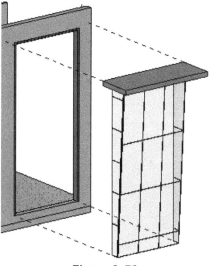

Figure 3–73

a. Draw them using ⌐ (Detail Line).

b. Draw them using ⌐ (Model Line).

c. Select the displaced element, click ⬚ (Edit), and draw them.

d. Select the displaced element, click ⟋ (Path), and select the corners of the displaced element.

5. How do you change the time of day when working with the Sun Path shown in Figure 3–74? (Select all that apply.)

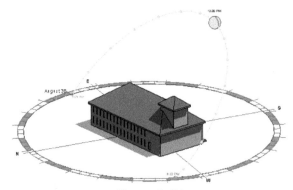

Figure 3–74

a. Modify the Sun Path Properties.

b. Drag the sun along the path.

c. Change the time in the Options Bar.

d. Click on the time control.

6. To get the most accurate view of how the sun impacts your project, which of the following must be set before a solar study is produced? (Select all that apply.)

a. The geographic location of the project site.

b. The orientation of a view to True North.

c. The rotation of the building in the project to True North.

d. The position of True North.

7. When creating a Multi-Day Sun Study, the Time Interval can be set to every 15 minutes.

a. True

b. False

Command Summary

Button	Command	Location
	Camera	• **Ribbon:** *View* tab>Create panel, expand 3D View • **Quick Access Toolbar:** expand 3D View
N/A	Graphic Display Options	• **Properties** • **View Control Bar: Expand Visual Styles** • **Shortcut:** GD
	Location	• **Ribbon:** *Manage* tab>Project Location panel
N/A	Preview Solar Study	• **View Control Bar:** Expand Sun Path
	Rotate True North	• **Ribbon:** *Manage* tab>Project Location panel, expand Position
	Shadows On	• **View Control Bar**
	Shadows Off	• **View Control Bar**
	Sun Path On	• **View Control Bar**
	Sun Path Off	• **View Control Bar**
N/A	Sun Settings	• **View Control Bar:** Expand Sun Path

Exploded Views

Button	Command	Location
	Displace Elements	• **Ribbon:** *Modify <elements type>* tab>View panel>Displace Elements
	Edit	• **Ribbon:** *Modify	Displacement Set* tab>Displacement Set panel>Edit
	Highlight Displacement Sets	• **View Control Bar**
	Path	• **Ribbon:** *Modify	Displacement Set* tab>Displacement Set panel>Path
	Reset	• **Ribbon:** *Modify	Displacement Set* tab>Displacement Set panel>Reset

Chapter 4

Rendering

The most powerful way to show off a design is to create a rendering. Renderings provide a "real world" view that typical floor plans and elevations cannot match. Using a rendering, you can show materials, lighting, daylight, people, furniture, and plants as a part of your design. You can use graduating levels of quality in your rendering as you prepare the view for a final, photorealistic rendering.

Learning Objectives in this Chapter

- Create a rendering of a view or a portion of a view.
- Set the rendering options.
- Add light fixtures and view light sources.
- Set up groups of lights so that you can control the lights that display in a rendering.
- Add people, plants, and other components to enhance your renderings.

4.1 Producing Basic Renderings

Rendering is a powerful tool where you display a photorealistic view of the model you are working on, such as the example shown in Figure 4–1. This can be used to help clients and designers alike to understand the building design in better detail. Renderings can be used as presentations for everything from code compliance to color schemes.

Figure 4–1

- While you can produce fairly elaborate renderings directly in the Autodesk® Revit® software, more extensive renderings are typically created in other software such as Autodesk® 3ds Max® or Autodesk Showcase.

To have access, you must be signed in using your Autodesk account.

- If you have an Autodesk Subscription, you can also render in the cloud using Autodesk A360 Rendering. The service will notify you when the rendering is complete. You can view, download, and modify completed renderings in the Render Gallery.

- All rendering done in Autodesk Revit is created using Autodesk Raytracer. This rendering engine accurately represents real-world materials by calculating light and its impact on materials as accurately as possible.

- If you are upgrading a model from previous versions, any Mental Ray settings are automatically mapped to the appropriate Raytracer settings. These settings are not maintained when upgrading.

Prepare Views for Rendering

To prepare a view for rendering, you need to:

- Create the 3D view.

- Verify that the materials you want are applied to the model elements.

- Toggle on shadows.

- Add lights and/or specify sun settings.

- Apply a background.

- Add RPC (Rich Photographic Content) components (such as plants, people, and cars).

> **Hint: Rendering 2D Views**
>
> Although only 3D views can be rendered, you can create a 3D view that looks like a 2D view. In a 3D view, right-click on the ViewCube and select **Orient to View** or **Orient to a Direction**. Set the view up using shadows and materials and render it, as shown in Figure 4–2.
>
>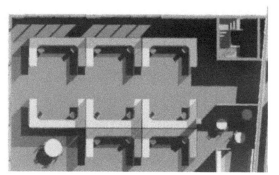
>
> Figure 4–2

- Materials and lighting are built into many of the elements in the Autodesk Revit model, including walls, windows, and light fixtures.

- The ⬜ (Realistic) Visual Style gives you a sense of what the rendered view might actually look like. It includes any RPC (Rich Photographic Content) you might have added.

Ray Trace takes time and computer power. Use it only when required.

- The ⬜ (Ray Trace) Visual Style puts you in the Interactive Ray Trace Mode, where you can zoom, pan, and rotate around the view while displaying the rendered materials.

How To: Render a view - Basic Steps

This option only displays if you are in a 3D view.

1. In the View Control Bar, click 🖾 (Show Rendering Dialog), enter **RR**, or in the *View* tab> Graphics panel, click

   ☕ (Render).

2. In the Rendering dialog box shown in Figure 4–3, set up the Rendering Settings for: *Quality*, *Output Settings*, *Lighting*, and *Background*.

Figure 4–3

3. Click **Render**.

4. The Rendering Progress dialog box opens, as shown in Figure 4–4. It closes when the rendering is complete, if that option is selected.

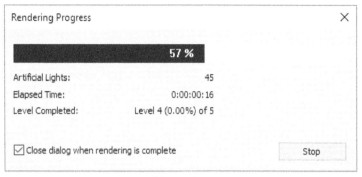

Figure 4–4

5. In the *Image* area of the Rendering dialog box, click **Adjust Exposure...** to modify the brightness and other options.

6. Click **Save to Project** to keep a copy of the rendering. Enter a name in the Save To Project dialog box (as shown in Figure 4–5) and click **OK**.

Saving a rendering to a project significantly increases the file size.

Figure 4–5

- Rendered views saved to the Project Browser can be printed and placed on sheets.

*The **Save to Project** and **Export** options are not available until a view is rendered.*

7. Click **Export...** to export a rendering as BMP, JPG, JPEG, PNG, or TIFF files.
   - The new file can be brought back into the project using the **Image** command.

8. When you are finished with an on-screen rendering, click **Show the model** in the *Display* area to remove the rendering from the view.

- Rendering information is saved with the view. In Properties, in the *Camera* area beside *Rendering Settings*, click **Edit...** to bring up the Rendering Settings dialog box, as shown in Figure 4–6. You can modify the *Quality*, *Lighting*, *Background*, and adjust the exposure of the *Image*.

Figure 4–6

- Rendering Settings can be included in a View Template and applied to other views.

Hint: Best Practices: Rendering a Region

The amount of time required to render an image is directly related to the complexity of the model and of the materials, the number of artificial lights, and the size or resolution of the image. To save time when you are developing the image, in the Render dialog box, select **Region** and place a region around some of the elements, as shown in Figure 4–7.

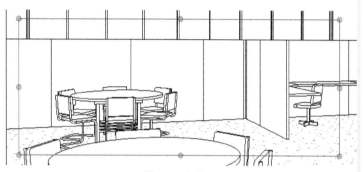

Figure 4–7

- Drag the box to move the entire region or drag the controls to resize the region.

- If some elements do not render as expected, check the materials. The material might be set to **<By Category>** rather than using a specific material.

Rendering Settings

Quality

The first setting you need to specify for a rendering is the *Quality*. You can select from a preset list (as shown in Figure 4–8) or create your own Custom (view specific) settings.

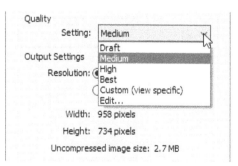

Figure 4–8

- Start with a draft quality image to verify that the materials and lights appear as you expect. Then, modify these elements and other settings and move to higher quality outputs as you create a more realistic image. Only use high quality settings when you know you have the image you want.

Output Settings

Renderings can be sent to the screen or to a printer. If you select the **Printer** option, you can select from a list of DPI (dots per inch) options. The *Width* and *Height* of the view are displayed in pixels and the image size is displayed in megabytes (MB), as shown in Figure 4–9.

Figure 4–9

Lighting

In the *Lighting* area in the Rendering dialog box, you can select a *Scheme* that defines the use of the sun and artificial light, set up the *Sun* settings, and work with the artificial lights in the model, as shown in Figure 4–10.

Figure 4–10

- Select from a variety of lighting schemes including **Exterior: Sun only**, **Exterior: Sun and Artificial**, **Exterior: Artificial only**, **Interior: Sun only**, **Interior: Sun and Artificial**, **Interior: Artificial only**.

- For the *Sun Setting*, click ⬚ (Browse) to access the dialog box to select, make, or edit other solar studies.

- Click **Artificial Lights...** to set up the lights and light groups used in the rendering.

Background

A360 rendering includes other backgrounds such as a field, riverbank, and seaport.

In the *Background* area in the Rendering dialog box, you can set the *Style* for the sky. Select from several levels of cloud cover, a color, or an image, and specify the *Haze* level for any amount of clouds, as shown in Figure 4–11.

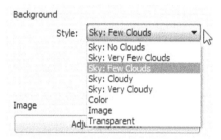

Figure 4–11

- The amount of clouds in a background impacts the overall quality of light in the rendering.

- When you select **Image**, you can specify any image file as the background.

- The **Transparent** option enables you to create a PNG or TIFF file that leaves the background transparent.

Image

Click **Adjust Exposure...** to open the Exposure Control dialog box, as shown in Figure 4–12. You can make the rendering brighter or darker, cooler or warmer, and more gray or more intense.

Figure 4–12

- Once you adjust the exposure, the Autodesk Revit software remembers the settings for the current view the next time you repeat the rendering process.

Display

The *Display* area in the Rendering dialog box displays **Show the model** when a rendering is active and **Show the rendering** when a rendering has been saved to the view, but is not *on* at the moment.

Hint: Saving Custom Rendering Settings

If you have modified the rendering settings quality, you can save the settings to a view template, which can be used in another view or project.

1. Set up the 3D view with the rendering settings. Only 3D views display Render Settings.
2. Right-click on the view name in the Project Browser and select **Create View Template From View...**.
3. Enter a new name for the view template and click **OK**.
4. In the View Templates dialog box (shown in Figure 4–13), verify that the *Render Settings* are correct.

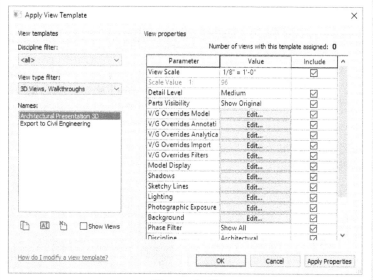

Figure 4–13

5. Click OK.

- To use the view settings for another view in the current project, right-click on the view name in the Project Browser and select **Apply Template Properties**.

- To use the view settings in another project, in the *Manage* tab>Settings panel, click (Transfer Project Standards). You must be in a plan view to transfer the standards.

Practice 4a

Produce Basic Renderings

Practice Objectives

- Render a region of a view in Draft mode to test the materials.
- Modify materials and render at Medium mode.

In this practice, you will set up and render a test region of a view. You will also modify the materials of some elements and test the rendering again at a slightly higher quality.

Task 1 - Render a Region of the View.

1. In the practice files folder, open **Midrise-Rendering.rvt**.

2. Open the 3D Views: **Front Perspective** view.

3. Set the *Visual Style* to ▱ (Shaded) to see the materials that come with the element styles (such as the brick walls, glass curtain wall and windows, and grass on the site), as shown in Figure 4–14.

Your view might look slightly different.

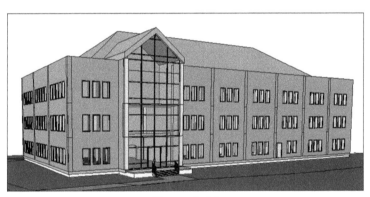

Figure 4–14

4. In the View Control Bar, click ☁ (Show Rendering Dialog).

5. In the Rendering dialog box, select **Region**. Modify the region in the view so it is similar to Figure 4–15.

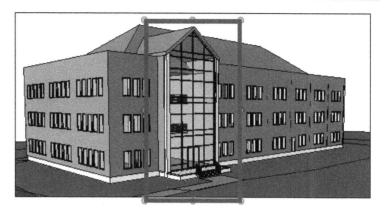

Figure 4–15

6. Set the following options in the Rendering dialog box:

- *Quality:* **Draft**
- *Output Settings:* **Screen**
- *Lighting:* Exterior: **Sun only**
- *Background:* Sky: **Few Clouds**

7. Click **Render**.

Task 2 - Modify Materials and Render the View again.

---

1. Using the Draft quality setting displays the materials, but is not clear enough to provide a good view of the building, especially the mullions of the curtain wall. However, you can see that the stairs are made of brick, where they should be showing a stone material.

2. Click **Show the model** to return to the unrendered perspective.

3. Select the stairs. In Properties, click 🔳 (Edit Type).

4. Set the *Tread, Riser,* and *Stringer Material* for the stairs to **Masonry-Stone**, as shown in Figure 4–16.

Materials and Finishes		☆
Tread Material	Masonry - Stone	
Riser Material	Masonry - Stone	
Stringer Material	Masonry - Stone	⋯
Monolithic Material	<By Category>	

Figure 4–16

5. Click **OK** to close the dialog box.

6. In the Rendering dialog box, set the *Quality Setting* to **Medium** and click **Render**.

7. The stairs display the correct color and the medium setting displays the curtain wall mullions more precisely, as shown in Figure 4–17. Adjust the exposure to brighten the rendering as required.

Figure 4–17

8. Save the rendering to the project as **Entry-Medium**.

9. Save the project.

4.2 Working with Lighting

A crucial component of rendering is setting up lights —both sunlight and light fixtures that radiate light, as shown in Figure 4–18. Sunlight is controlled by the location, time of day, and cloud cover. Artificial light comes from lighting components that are added to the reflected ceiling plan or floor plan.

Figure 4–18

Light Fixture Families

Light fixtures are families that are placed with (Component). Many of the light fixture families included with the Autodesk Revit software have multiple options for the type of lamp in the fixture, as shown in Figure 4–19.

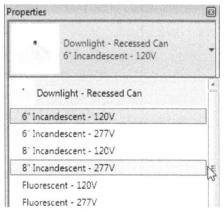

Figure 4–19

Viewing Light Sources

As you place light fixtures, especially spotlights, sconces, or downlights illuminating specific objects, it is helpful to toggle on the light sources, as shown in Figure 4–20.

Figure 4–20

How To: Toggle On Light Sources

1. Open the Visibility/Graphic Overrides dialog box.
2. In the *Model Categories* tab, expand **Lighting Fixtures** and select **Light Source**, as shown in Figure 4–21.

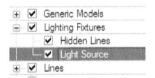

Figure 4–21

3. Click **OK**.

- Toggle on the ⬜ (Shaded) Visual Style to get the best view of the light sources. Shading displays the difference between the beam angle and the field angle for spotlights.

- To have even more accurate lighting in a rendering, you can specify photometric light sources. These sources use an IES file from the lighting manufacturer. This file describes the light intensity for points on a spherical grid and how the light comes from the fixture. Light sources are specified in the lighting fixture family.

Setting Up Light Groups

While a project might include hundreds of light fixtures in the building, only some of them impact the rendering you are working on. To save time, limit the light fixtures to those that are used in the current view by creating and setting up light groups.

How To: Add Lights to a Light Group

1. Open the reflected ceiling plan view that displays the lights you want to group.
2. Select at least one of the lights.
3. In the Options Bar, in the Light Group drop-down list, select an existing group or select **Edit/New...** to create a new group, as shown in Figure 4–22.

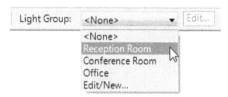

Figure 4–22

4. If you select an existing group, an alert box opens prompting you that you are about to move the selected light(s) to a new light group. Click **OK**.
5. If you select **Edit/New...**, the Artificial Lights dialog box opens, as shown in Figure 4–23.

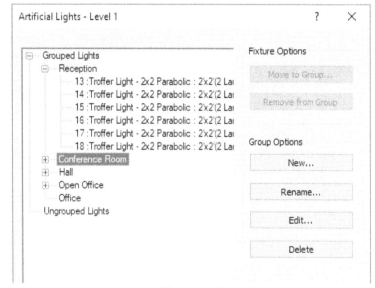

Figure 4–23

6. In the *Group Options* area in the dialog box, click **New** to create a new group.
7. In the New Light Group dialog box, enter a name for the light group and click **OK**.
8. Select the new group name and in the *Group Options* area, click **Edit...**
9. The Light Group panel displays with the **Add** button selected. Click on each light that you want to add to the light group, as shown in Figure 4–24.

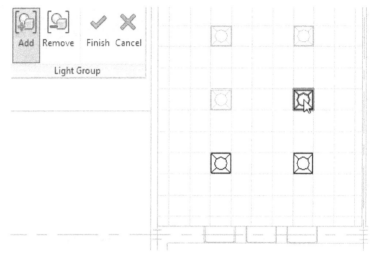

Figure 4–24

10. Click (Finish) and then click **OK**.

• When you want to add lights to an existing light group, select at least one light. In the Options Bar, select a Light Group from the drop-down list (as shown in Figure 4–25), and click **Edit...**.

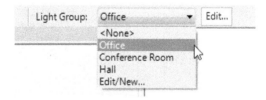

Figure 4–25

How To: Use Light Groups in a Rendering

1. Open a 3D view to render. In the View Control Bar, click

   📷 (Show Rendering Dialog).
2. In the Rendering dialog box, in the *Lighting* area, select a *Scheme* that includes artificial lights.
3. Click **Artificial Lights...**.

This option is only available if a Scheme with artificial lights has been selected.

4. In the Artificial Lights dialog box for the view, the lists of grouped and ungrouped lights display. Clear the groups and ungrouped lights that you do not need for the rendering, as shown in Figure 4–26.

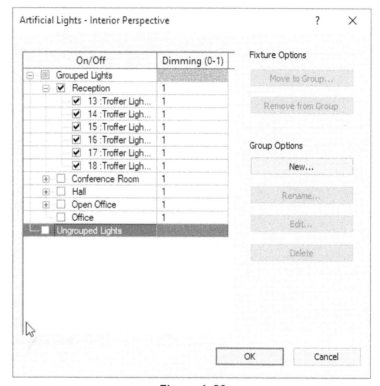

Figure 4–26

• You can also dim a light or light group using this dialog box. Set the value for *Dimming* between **0** (off) and **1** (not dimmed).

Hint: Section Boxes and Rendering

Section boxes are another way to limit the geometry viewed and calculated when creating a rendering.

In a 3D view, in the *Extents* area in the Properties dialog box, click **Section Box**. The default size is the extents of the view. Resize the section box using the controls, as shown in Figure 4–27.

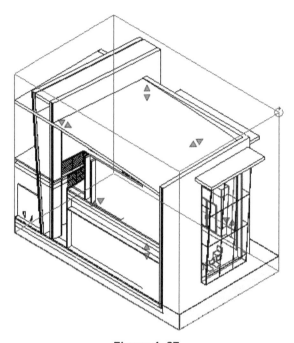

Figure 4–27

- Open the view you want to render and ensure that **Section Box** is on in this view as well.

Practice 4b

Work with Lighting

Practice Objectives

- Set up light groups for a specific room and add light fixtures.
- Render a view using light groups.

In this practice, you will set up light groups, add a light fixture, view the light source, and render a region. Once the rendering is finished, you will adjust the exposure, as shown in Figure 4–28.

Original Rendering   *Exposure Adjusted*

Figure 4–28

Task 1 - Set Up Light Groups.

1. Continue working in **Midrise-Rendering.rvt**.

2. Open the Ceiling Plans: **Level 1** view. Some light fixtures have been added to the project, as shown in Figure 4–29.

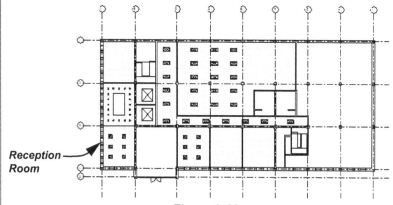

Reception — Room

Figure 4–29

3. Zoom in on the Reception Room in the lower left corner of the building.

4. Select one of the lights. In the Options Bar, in the Light Group drop-down list, select **Edit/New**.

5. In the Artificial Lights dialog box, in the *Group Options* area, click **New**. Set the name to **Reception** and click **OK**. Click **OK** to close the dialog box.

6. Select all six lights in the Reception Room and set the *Light Group* to **Reception**, as shown in Figure 4–30.

Figure 4–30

7. Click **OK** to move the lights to the Light Group. Click in empty space to clear the selection of the lights.

Task 2 - Add Light Fixtures.

---

1. Open the Floor Plans: **Level 1** view and zoom in on the Reception room.

2. In the *Architecture* tab>Build panel, click ⬚ (Component).

3. In the *Modify | Place Component* tab>Mode panel, click

   ⬚ (Load Family).

4. In the Load Family dialog box, select the *Lighting> Architectural>Internal* folder. Select one of the **Floor Lamp** components and load it into the project.

5. Place the lamp behind the chairs near the outside corner of the wall. Rotate it as required, as shown in Figure 4–31.

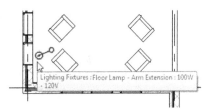

Figure 4–31

6. Select the floor lamp. In the Options Bar, set the *Light Group* to **Reception**.

7. Open the **3D Views: Interior Perspective** view.

8. View the light sources. Enter **VG** and expand the *Lighting Fixtures* category. Select **Light Source** and click **OK**.

9. In the View Status Bar, click ⬛ (Shaded). The lights sources display similar to those shown in Figure 4–32, depending on the floor lamp you selected.

Figure 4–32

Task 3 - Render a view.

---

1. In the View Control Bar, click 🔆 (Show Rendering Dialog).

2. In the Rendering dialog box, in the *Lighting* area, set the *Scheme* to **Interior: Sun and Artificial**.

3. Beside *Sun Setting*, click ⬚ (Choose a sun location).

4. In the Sun Settings dialog box, *Solar Study* area, select **Still**.

5. In the *Settings* area, set the *Time* to early morning. This keeps the light coming in from the windows from being too bright. Click **OK**.

6. Click **Artificial Lights....**

---

7. In the Artificial Lights dialog box, verify that **Reception** is toggled on and **Ungrouped Lights** is cleared so that they do not display in the rendering, as shown in Figure 4–33.

Figure 4–33

8. Click **OK**.

9. In the Rendering dialog box, select **Region**. Modify the region so that it shows the floor lamp and some other light fixture.

10. Set the *Quality Setting* to **Draft** and click **Render**.

11. When the Rendering Progress dialog box opens, check the number of Artificial Lights it is calculating, as shown in Figure 4–34.

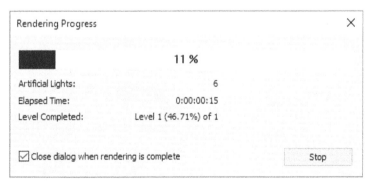

Figure 4–34

12. When the rendering displays, click **Adjust Exposure...** and modify the various exposure controls as required.

13. Save the project.

4.3 Enhancing Renderings

Many components provided in the Autodesk Revit software are ready to be rendered. Although furniture has a specific wood pattern, lights include light sources, and windows have transparent glass material in the panes, this is often not enough. You can further enhance renderings by splitting faces and applying different materials to elements such as walls and floors. You can also add RPC (Rich Photorealistic Content) components, such as trees and people, that are specifically created for adding to renderings, as shown in Figure 4–35.

Figure 4–35

Applying Materials

You may want to apply information that is not in the model element, such as different materials on the face of a wall, as shown in Figure 4–36. The **Split Face** command divides an element face into smaller separate faces. You can then use the **Paint** command to apply different materials to the faces.

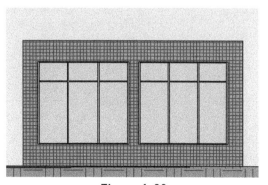

Figure 4–36

*If the **Select elements by face** option is toggled on, you can click directly on the face.*

- The changes made with **Split Face** and **Paint** are displayed in elevations and 3D views.

- The area and other information about the materials can be used in a Material takeoff schedule.

How To: Create a Split Face

1. Switch to an elevation view (a 3D view works as well).

2. In the *Modify* tab>Geometry panel, click 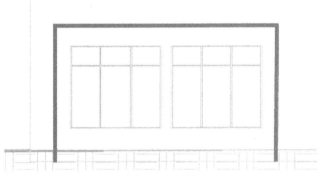 (Split Face).

3. Select the edge of the face that you want to modify. Use <Tab> as required, to toggle through the available faces.

4. In the *Modify | Split Face>Create Boundary* tab>Draw panel, use the sketch tools to create a sketch as required to define the split, as shown in Figure 4–37.

Figure 4–37

- The split must be a closed shape completely inside the face, or an open shape that touches the face edges.

- Windows are cut out of faces automatically.

5. Click ✓ (Finish Edit Mode).

- Before you begin working with split faces, ensure that the walls are mitered. By default, the walls are butted to each other. This creates a problem when you select faces.

- To save time, use a wall style that includes the primary material you want to use on the split face. For example, if you are working with brick, set the wall to a type that has a brick face. This way, you can work with the brick courses when creating the split face.

- When using a material, such as brick, you can snap to the pattern and even lock the split lines to the pattern, as shown in Figure 4–38.

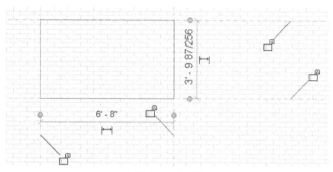

Figure 4–38

You can double-click on the edge of the split face lines to switch to the Edit Boundary mode. If you double-click on the face (with the **Select elements by face** option toggled on) it switches to the Edit Profile mode, which impacts the entire wall, not just the split face boundary

How To: Apply Material with Paint

1. In the *Modify* tab>Geometry panel, click (Paint) or enter **PT**.
2. In the Material Browser, select a material. You can run a search or filter the list using specific types of materials, as shown in Figure 4–39.

The browser remains open as you apply the paint.

Material Browser - Acoustic Ceiling Tile 24 x 24

Search

Project Materials: All

<All>
Carpet
Concrete
Gas
Generic
Glass
Masonry
Metal
Miscellaneous
Paint
Plastic
System
Textile
Unassigned
Wood

Table Top   Teak   Textile - Black

Textile - Slate Blue   Tile, Mosaic, Gray   Tile, Porce..., 4in

Figure 4–39

3. Hover the cursor over the face you want to paint. It should highlight, as shown in Figure 4–40. Click on the face to apply the material.

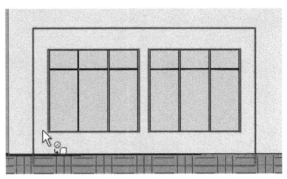

Figure 4–40

4. Continue selecting materials and painting other faces as required.

5. In the Material Browser, click **Done** to finish the command.

- Some material patterns display as shaded when you zoom out. Zoom in to display the pattern. Other material patterns only display when you are in the ⊟ (Realistic) Visual Style or when you render.

- To remove the material applied to a face, in the *Modify* tab> Geometry panel, expand ⊡ (Paint) and click ⊡ (Remove Paint). Select the face(s) from which you want to remove the material.

Adding People and Other Components

Rich Photorealistic Content (RPC) is a specific type of component that helps to make renderings more lifelike. The Autodesk Revit libraries include RPC people and plants, as shown in Figure 4–41, as well as office items and vehicles. To place signs, paintings, and other flat graphics such as the picture in Figure 4–41, you can add decals.

Figure 4–41

Adding RPC elements

RPC elements are added using the **Component** command. Samples of vehicles, people, and office objects are available in the Library in the *Entourage* folder. Once you load them into the project, you can select them from the Type Selector, as shown in Figure 4–42.

You can purchase additional objects from .ArchVision^{TM}

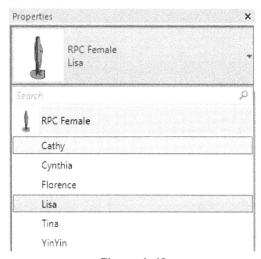

Figure 4–42

- You need to be in a 3D orthographic view or floor plan view to place components.

In a plan, the person displays with a point indicating the direction in which they are facing. In a 3D view, they display in outline. In a rendering, they display as they have been created, as shown in Figure 4–43.

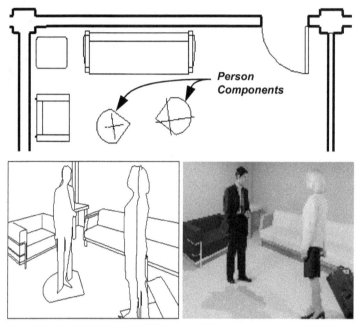

Figure 4–43

- If you are working with Autodesk Revit topography elements components such as trees and shrubs, you need to use a different command that places the element directly on the toposurface. In the *Massing & Site* tab> Model Site panel, click ⬆ (Site Component).

Adding Decals

Decals are links to images that you can place on flat or cylindrical surfaces. They are used for signs, pictures, or other flat surfaced elements. Decals display an outline in most visual styles (as shown in Figure 4–44); however, they display in full when rendered or in the Realistic visual style, as shown in Figure 4–45.

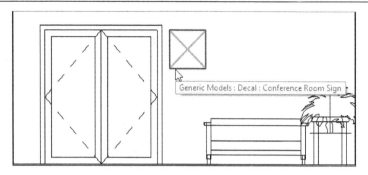

Figure 4–44

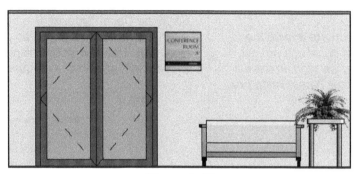

Figure 4–45

How To: Add Decals

1. Open a 2D view such as a section or elevation.

2. In the *Insert* tab>Link panel, expand 🗗 (Decal) and click 🗗 (Place Decal).

3. In the Type Selector, select a decal.

4. Place the decal on the face of an element.

5. In the Options Bar, specify the *Width* and *Height*. Click **Lock Proportions** if you want to change one and have the other resize proportionally, as shown in Figure 4–46. Click **Reset** to return to the original size.

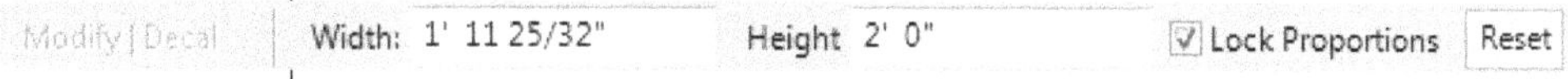

| Modify | Decal | Width: 1' 11 25/32" | Height 2' 0" | ☑ Lock Proportions | Reset |

Figure 4–46

- You can also use the *Drag* controls to resize the decal.

How To: Create a Decal Type

1. Start the **Decal** command.
   - If no decal exists in the project, in the Decal Types dialog box, click (Create New Decal), set a name for it, and skip to step 6.
2. In the Type Selector, select a Decal and click **Edit Type**.
3. In the Type Properties dialog box, click **Duplicate...**.
4. In the Name dialog box, enter a name for the decal and click **OK**.
5. Beside the **Decal Attributes** parameter, click **Edit...**
6. In the Decal Types dialog box beside *Source*, click .
7. In the Select File dialog box, select the image and click **Open**. The new image displays and you can modify the other settings, as shown in Figure 4–47.

If you are adding the first decal in a project, you will work in the full Decal Types dialog box.

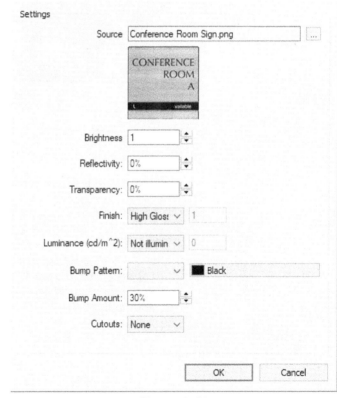

Figure 4–47

8. Click **OK**.
- To open the full Decal Types dialog box, in the *Insert* tab>Link panel, expand (Decal) and click (Decal Types).

Practice 4c

Enhance Renderings

Practice Objectives

- Modify the floor materials by splitting the face and painting a new material on part of it
- Add a decal to a surface.
- Add people and plant components in a room and render it.

In this practice, you will split the face of the floor and apply a different material to a part of it. You will also add a sign to the reception desk and add people and trees. You will then render it, as shown in Figure 4–48.

Figure 4–48

Task 1 - Modify the floor material.

1. Continue working in **Midrise-Rendering.rvt**.

2. Open the **Floor Plans: Level 1** view.

3. Zoom in on the reception room in the lower left part of the building.

4. In the *Modify | Floors* tab>Geometry panel, click 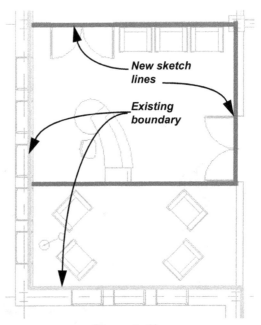 (Split Face.

5. Hover the cursor over the interior edge of one of the exterior walls and select the floor.

6. In the *Modify | Split Face>Create Boundary* tab>Draw panel, use the draw tools to split the reception room floor into two faces, as shown in Figure 4–49. You can model the design, as required. Click (Finish Edit Mode) when you are done.

The sketch must be closed or touch existing boundary lines to make the closed shape.

New sketch lines

Existing boundary

Figure 4–49

7. Set the *Visual Style* to **Realistic**. The existing floor type includes a burgandy carpet.

8. In the *Modify* tab>Geometry panel, click (Paint).

9. In the Material Browser, select a material for part of the floor. A variety of carpet styles are available in the project, as shown in Figure 4–50. There are also a number of *Wood* project materials that you can chose from.

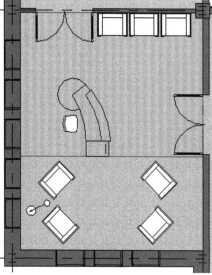

Figure 4–50   **Figure 4–51**

10. Click **Done**.

11. If required, you can change the other part of the floor, as shown in Figure 4–51.

   • To keep the **Paint** command from changing the rest of the carpeting in the building, you need to create a second split face.

12. Open the **Interior Perspective** view and test out the carpet flooring change by setting the *Visual Style* to **Ray Trace**.

13. Modify the view angle if required, to show the floor.

14. Close **Interactive Ray Trace**.

15. Save the project.

Task 2 - Add a Decal

1. Return to the **Floor Plans: Level 1** view.

2. Add a section that will display the front of the reception desk.

3. To make the desk easier to see in elevation, modify the section so it is close to the desk, as shown in Figure 4–52.

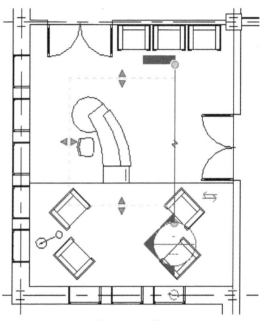

Figure 4–52

*The desk does not display when the Detail Level is set to **Coarse**.*

4. Open the view and set the *Detail Level* to **Fine**.

5. Zoom in on the reception desk.

6. In the *Insert* tab>Link panel, click (Decal).

7. In the Decal Types dialog box, click (Create New Decal) and name it **Conference Room Sign**.

8. In the Decal Types dialog box beside *Source*, click .

9. In the Select File dialog box, navigate to the practice files folder and select **Conference Room Sign.png**. Click **Open**. The new image displays and you can modify the other settings, as shown in Figure 4–53.

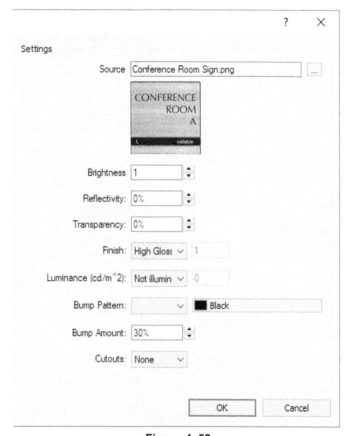

Figure 4–53

10. Place the sign on the face of the desk.

11. Click **Modify** and select the new decal.

12. In the Options Bar, verify that **Lock Proportions** is selected. Change the *Height* to **1'-0"**.

13. Click in the *Width* edit box to apply the change.

14. Change the *Visual Style* to **Realistic** to see the final image. Move the decal where you want it on the desk, such as that shown in Figure 4–54.

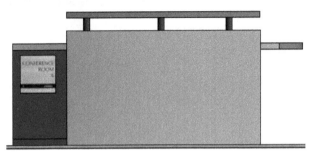

Figure 4–54

If you want to place the decal on a different part of the desk, you need to delete it and reapply it.

15. Save the project.

Task 3 - Add People and Plants.

---

1. Return to the **Floor Plans: Level 1** view.

2. In the *Architecture* tab>Build panel, click ▱ (Component).

3. In the *Modify | Place Component* tab>Mode panel, click

   ▱ (Load Family).

4. In the Library, in the *Entourage* folder, select **RCP Male.rfa** and **RCP Female.rfa** and load them into the project. In the *Planting* folder, select and load **RCP Tree - Conifer.rfa** and **RCP Tree - Deciduous.rfa**.

5. Place several people inside the Reception Room in the floor plan. Rotate them as required. The pointed end is the front of the person, as shown in Figure 4–55.

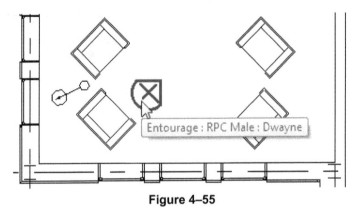

Figure 4–55

There is a toposurface in this project.

6. In the *Massing & Site* tab>Model Site panel, click (Site Component).

7. Add trees outside the windows so that they can be seen in the perspective view.

8. Switch to the **Interior Perspective** view. You should see outlines of the people and possibly some of the trees through the window, similar to that shown in Figure 4–56.

Figure 4–56

9. Switch to the (Realistic) visual style to test the direction of the people.

10. Render a region or if time permits, the entire scene.

11. Save the project.

Chapter Review Questions

1. What should you do to prepare a view for rendering?

   a. Toggle on the **Sun Path**.

   b. Lock the view.

   c. Add lights.

   d. Set the *Visual Style* to 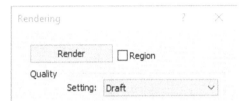 (Realistic).

2. What is the purpose of the **Region** option in the Rendering dialog box, as shown in Figure 4–57?

   Figure 4–57

   a. It only toggles on lights in a specified region.

   b. It only displays materials in a specified region.

   c. It only includes shadows in a specified region.

   d. It only renders in a specified region.

3. If a rendering is darker than expected, how do you make it lighter?

   a. Add more light fixtures.

   b. Adjust the exposure.

   c. Modify the location of the sun.

   d. Change the *Lighting Scheme*.

4. How do you limit the number of lights used in a rendering?

   a. Hide any lights that you do not want to use.

   b. Isolate the lights that you want to use.

   c. Set up a Light Group.

   d. Delete the additional lights.

5. How can you display the light sources, as shown in Figure 4–58?

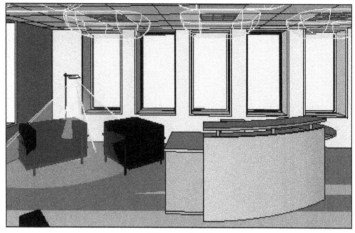

Figure 4–58

a. Set the *Visual Style* to (Ray Trace).

b. In the Visibility/Graphics dialog box, select **Light Source**.

c. In Properties, select **Light Source**.

d. It depends on the type of light fixture family used.

Command Summary

Button	Command	Location
	Component	• **Ribbon:** *Architecture* tab>Build panel • **Shortcut:** CM
	Decal Types	• **Ribbon:** *Insert* tab>Link panel, expand Decal
	Load Family	• **Ribbon:** *Modify | Place Component* tab> Mode panel
	Place Decal	• **Ribbon:** *Insert* tab>Link panel, expand Decal
	Site Component	• **Ribbon:** *Massing & Site* tab>Model Site panel
	Show Rendering Dialog	• **View Control Bar**
	Transfer Project Standards	• **Ribbon:** *Manage* tab>Settings panel

Additional Tools

There are many other tools available in the Autodesk® Revit® software that can be used when creating massing studies and visualizing models. This appendix provides details about several tools and commands that are related to those covered in this learning guide.

Learning Objectives in this Appendix

- Create materials and material libraries that can be used in multiple projects.
- Create and edit a perspective walkthrough.
- Review the process of creating a conceptual mass family, including dimensions, labels, and Family Types.
- Work with reference-based forms.

A.1 Creating Materials

When you shade or render Autodesk Revit models, their appearance depends on the materials that have been associated with the elements, as shown in a shaded view in Figure A–1. Materials also include information that can be used in material takeoff schedules and in energy and structural analysis. You can use materials supplied with the Autodesk Revit software or create custom materials.

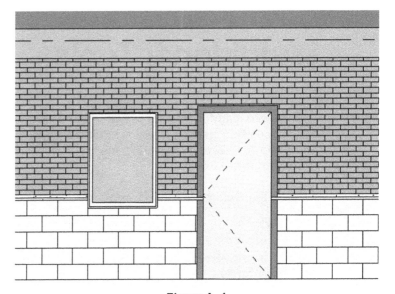

Figure A–1

- Materials can be assigned in several ways: using ⟨Paint⟩ on faces, setting it in the layers of system families (such as walls and floors), and in object styles. You also assign materials when you create other component families, such as doors and furniture.

Materials consist of 2D graphic settings for shading, surface, and cut patterns and the 3D rendering appearance, as well as physical and thermal properties. You can also include identity data, such as manufacturer, model, and keynotes.

Material Libraries

Materials are stored in libraries, which can be shared between Autodesk Revit projects and the AutoCAD, Autodesk® Inventor®, Showcase and Autodesk® 3ds Max® software. Before creating custom materials it is recommended that you create a custom library. Materials can be copied between the current project and the library.

*   You can also use Transfer Project Standards to bring in all the materials from another project into the current project.

*   Older versions of materials may need to be updated with appearance assets, as shown in Figure A–2. All legacy materials still work but they may not be as complex and nuanced when rendering.

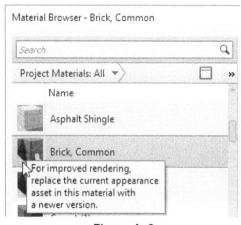

Figure A–2

How To: Create a Material Library

1. In the *Manage* tab>Settings panel, click ⚬ (Materials).

2. At the bottom of the Material Browser, expand 📄 (Creates, opens and edits user-defined libraries) and select **Create New Library**, as shown in Figure A–3.

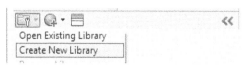

Figure A–3

3. In the Select File dialog box, navigate to the appropriate folder, type a *File name* and save the library. The Material Library displays in the Library list without any materials displayed.

4. Create new materials as required in the current project. Then drag and drop both new and existing materials from the project materials into the new library, as shown in Figure A–4.

Libraries that come with the Autodesk Revit software are locked. You can copy materials from them but cannot add or change materials in them.

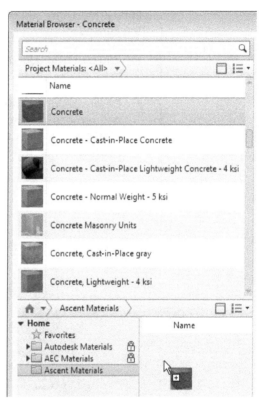

Figure A–4

How To: Create a Material

1. In the *Manage* tab>Settings panel, click ⊛ (Materials).

2. In the Material Editor, expand ⊕ (Creates or duplicates a material), and select either **Create New Material** or **Duplicate Material** as shown in Figure A–5. If you are duplicating a material, select an existing material similar to what you want to use first.

*You can also right-click on an existing material in the Material Browser and select **Duplicate**.*

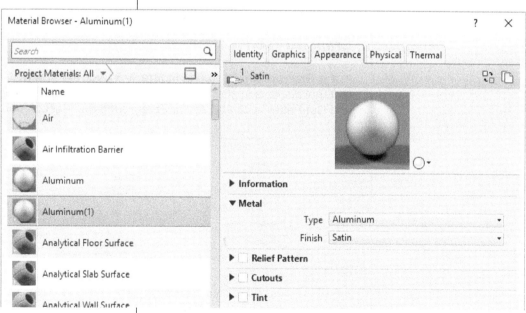

Create New Material
Duplicate Selected Material

Figure A–5

3. A new material is added to the current project. Modify the name of the material or right-click on the Material name in the Material Browser and select **Rename**.

   • Duplicated materials include all of the properties of the existing material as shown for a new Aluminum material in Figure A–6.

Figure A–6

4. Fill out the information on each of the tabs.
5. Click **Apply** and add additional materials as required.
6. Click **OK** when you are finished.

Identity Tab

In the *Identity* tab, you set up the *Descriptive Information*, *Product Information*, and *Revit Annotation Information* for the material, as shown in Figure A–7. This information can be used in material takeoff schedules.

Figure A–7

Graphics Tab

In the *Graphics* tab (shown in Figure A–8), you set how a material displays in shaded or hidden line mode. The Surface and Cut Patterns can be set for Foreground and Background.

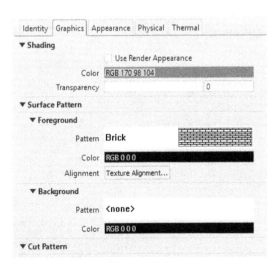

Figure A–8

- The *Shading* area controls how the material displays when an element is shaded. If you want the shaded view to resemble the rendered view, select **Use Render Appearance**. The color and other options are modified to match the Render Appearance selection. Alternatively, you can set up a color and transparency ratio. Only use this if the render appearance would be too dark or otherwise not suit the use.

The *Surface Pattern* and *Cut Pattern* areas enable you to select a fill pattern and color to display on a surface or in a section cut. Surface patterns stay true to size. Cut patterns are drafting patterns, which change size according to the view scale.

Appearance Tab

In the *Appearance* tab, you can set different aspects of a rendered material, including **Information**, the type of material (in this example Masonry is selected as shown in Figure A–9) and other parameters depending on the type of material you are working with. Note that changing the asset changes all of the information, so check if that is an option first.

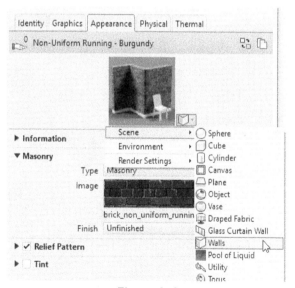

Figure A–9

- You can select how to display the preview of the material by expanding the Scene list next to the graphic, as shown in Figure A–9, above.

- You can modify the *Render Settings* of the preview to either **Draft Quality** or **Production Quality**.

- If you duplicate a material and then change asset-related information (such as the Image or Color) the original material also updates. To prevent this from happening, duplicate or change the asset before making changes.

Physical Tab

In the *Physical* tab, you can specify information about the physical properties of the material. The options vary by material type, as shown in Figure A–10.

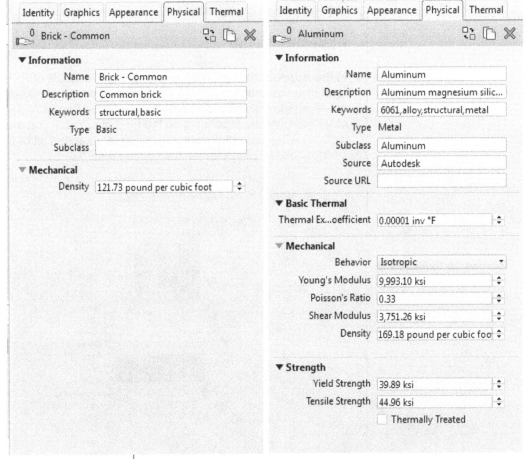

Figure A–10

- Some materials, such as **EPDM Membrane** or **Vapor Retarder**, do not have physical properties, but do have thermal properties.

- Analytical surface and Default materials do not have physical or thermal properties.

- As changing the asset changes all of the information, you should check to see if that is an option first.

Working with Assets

Physical Assets contain preset parameters for materials. These assets are available in the *Appearance*, *Physical* and *Thermal* tabs. Autodesk provides an extensive library of assets that are divided by material type, as shown in Figure A–11. You can modify and add assets to materials depending on the variables required in the project.

Figure A–11

Assets updated with higher rendering capabilities do not have a triangle in the lower left corner, as shown in Figure A–12.

Original Cherry Asset　　　　　*Updated Cherry Asset*

Figure A–12

How To: Replace an Asset for a Material

1. In the Material Browser, select the material that you want to modify.
2. In the *Appearance*, *Physical*, or *Thermal* tab, click ⬚ (Replaces this asset).
3. In the Asset Browser, hover the cursor over the required asset and click ⇄ (Replaces the current asset in the editor with this asset), as shown in Figure A–13.

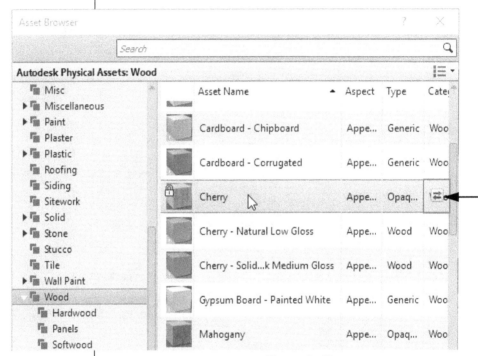

Figure A–13

4. Close the Asset Browser.

• The assets are filtered by type. Therefore, you need to modify the Appearance asset by clicking through the *Appearance* tab, etc.

• You can create new assets by duplicating an existing one and then modifying the parameters.

A.2 Creating Walkthroughs

A *Walkthrough* is a series of perspective views linked together in a path. You specify the location of *key frames*—specific points in the plan that create the path of the Walkthrough. Key frames are displayed as squares on the path, as shown in Figure A–14. A line shows the view direction. Once you create a Walkthrough, you can edit its individual frames and export the whole sequence to an AVI file.

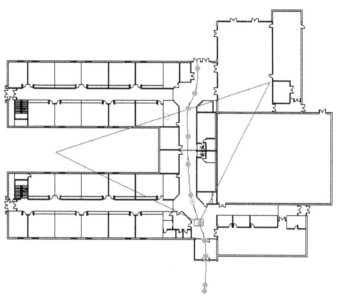

Figure A–14

How To: Create a Walkthrough

1. Open a plan view. Walkthroughs can be made in other views, but they are typically laid out in plan views.
2. In the *View* tab>Create panel (or Quick Access Toolbar), expand 🏠 (3D View) and click ‼ (Walkthrough).
3. In the Options Bar, set the perspective and offset from the level as required, as shown in Figure A–15.

Figure A–15

4. Click on the screen to place the first key frame.
5. Continue adding key frames as required. You can change the offset if required. For example, if you are walking up a set of stairs.
6. In the *Modify | Walkthrough* tab>Walkthrough panel, click

    (Finish Walkthrough). A Walkthrough view is created in the Project Browser with the default name of **Walkthrough1**.

- You can view and modify the walkthrough in either the plan view (to edit the path) or walkthrough view (to display the 3D views).

How To: View a Walkthrough

To see the camera and path in a plan view, right-click on the Walkthrough name in the Walkthrough section of the Project Browser and select Show Camera.

1. In the Project Browser, expand the **Walkthroughs** node and select the name of the walkthrough.
2. Click on the edge of the crop region.
3. In the *Modify | Cameras* tab>Walkthrough panel, click

    (Edit Walkthrough).
4. The *Edit Walkthrough* tab displays additional tools and the Options Bar displays the location controls, as shown in Figure A–16.

Figure A–16

5. Set the *Frame* number to **1**.

6. In the *Edit Walkthrough* tab>Walkthrough panel, click

    (Play).

Modifying a Walkthrough

When you are modifying a walkthrough, it can help to have both the walkthrough view and the plan view open at the same time. This enables you to see the 3D view and modify the path in the 2D view.

Controls	With the plan view active, select either **Active Camera**, **Path**, **Add Key Frame**, or **Remove Key Frame**. Then, modify the controls.
Frame #	Moves the cursor to the specified frame.
Arrow buttons	Use when you are viewing the Walkthrough to ensure that it displays the views you are expecting. You can select from ◃◃ (Previous Key Frame), ◃ (Previous Frame), ▹ (Next Frame), ▹▹ (Next Key Frame), and ▷ (Play). To stop playing, press \<Esc\> or click **Cancel** in the Status Bar.
👣	**Open Walkthrough** opens the specified frame. Modify the crop window in one frame, it modifies in all frames.
📷	**Reset Cameras.** If you move the direction of the camera in a frame, clicking this button to reset all of the changed camera directions to the original path.

- If you click in a view while editing a walkthrough, an alert box opens, prompting you to decide whether to continue editing the walkthrough.

Setting Walkthrough Frames

To upgrade the performance of the walkthrough and smooth out portions where the rate of change appears to be too fast, you can change the number of frames between key frames.

In Properties, scroll down to the *Other* section and click the button next to the *Walkthrough Frames* parameter, as shown in Figure A–17.

The button displays the number of frames in the walkthrough.

Other	⌃
Walkthrough Frames	300

Figure A–17

7. In the Walkthrough Frames dialog box (shown in Figure A–18), you can adjust the frame number, increment, or travel per frame. Clear the **Uniform Speed** option to change individual frame times.

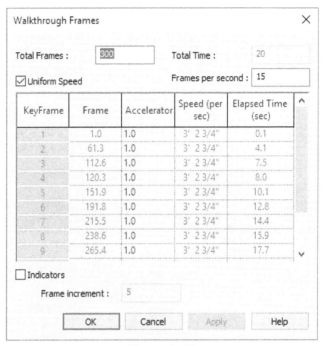

Figure A–18

How To: Export a Walkthrough

To show the Walkthrough outside the Autodesk Revit software, you need to create an AVI file.

1. Open the Walkthrough.

2. In the *File* tab, click ⬜ (Export)> ⬜ (Images and Animations)> 👣 (Walkthrough).

3. Fill out the Length/Format dialog box, as shown in Figure A–19. In the *Output Length* area, specify which frames you want to include and the number of frames per second. In the *Format* area, select how you want the movie to display. You can display in **Wireframe**, **Hidden Line**, **Shaded**, **Shaded with Edges**, **Consistent Colo**r, **Realistic**, and **Rendering**. Use the existing dimensions or specify a zoom scale factor.

Autodesk Raytracer settings are used if you are in the Rendering display.

Figure A–19

4. Click **OK**
5. In the Export Walkthrough dialog box, specify the folder and name for the new file.
6. Click **Save**.
7. In the Video Compression dialog box, select the format and quality and click **OK**. The Walkthrough displays as it creates the video file.

• You need significant computer resources (CPU and RAM) to produce AVI files.

Practice A1 | Create Walkthroughs

Practice Objective

- Create an interior walkthrough and edit it to display better views along the path.

In this practice, you will create a Walkthrough in a building, as shown in plan in Figure A–20.

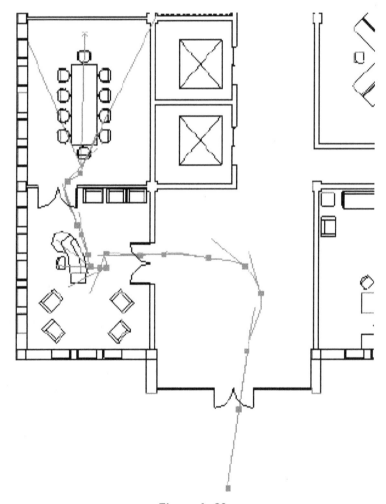

Figure A–20

Task 1 - Create an Interior walkthrough.

1. In the practice files folder, open **Midrise-Walkthrough.rvt**.

2. Open the **Floor Plans: Level 1** view.

3. In the *View* tab>Create panel (or Quick Access Toolbar),

   expand ⬠ (3D View) and click ❗❗ (Walkthrough).

4. Select points to create a path that comes in through the front entrance, then goes to the left side into the reception room and conference room, in which the furniture and ceilings have been configured.

5. After the last point, click ✓ (Finish Walkthrough).

Task 2 - Test and Edit the Walkthrough.

1. Open the **Walkthroughs: Walkthrough1** view and the **Floor Plans: Level 1** view. Tile these two views.

2. In the 3D view, select the edge of the crop region.

3. In the *Modify | Cameras* tab>Walkthrough panel, click

   ❗❗ (Edit Walkthrough).

4. In the Options Bar, set the *Frame* to **1**.

5. Return to the *Edit Walkthrough* tab>Walkthrough panel, click

   ▷ (Play).

6. Edit the Walkthrough as required. Adjust the camera at different frames or speed up the process through some turns.

7. If you have time and computer resources, create an AVI file of your Walkthrough.

A.3 Conceptual Mass Families

Conceptual Mass Families can be used to create massing studies that can then be used in a project. This is useful if you are creating multiple copies of one building design on a site, as shown in Figure A–21. As with other families, you can use reference planes, dimensions and labels, and types to make the mass elements parametric.

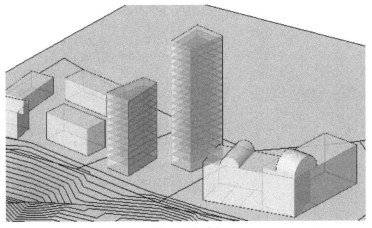

Figure A–21

How To: Create a Conceptual Mass Family

1. In the Home screen *Families* area, click **New...**, or in the *File* tab, expand (New) and click (Conceptual Mass).
2. In the New Conceptual Mass - Select Template File dialog box, in the *Conceptual Mass* folder, select the **Mass.rfa** template and click **Open**.
3. In the Conceptual Mass Environment, in the *Create* tab> Draw panel (shown in Figure A–22), add reference planes, reference lines, dimensions, labels, and other parameters, as required.
4. Use the drawing tools to draw the profiles and paths, as required.

Figure A–22

5. Select the sketched linework.

6. In the *Modify | Lines* tab>Form panel, click 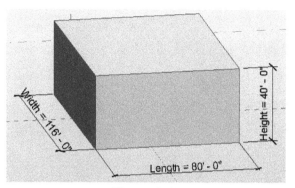 (Create Form). The Autodesk Revit software creates a 3D mass based on the selected linework.
7. Use the dimensioning tools to add additional labels, as shown in Figure A–23.

Figure A–23

8. In the *Modify* tab>Properties panel, click (Family Types). In the Family Types dialog box (shown in Figure A–24), set up formulas, additional parameters, and Family Types as required.

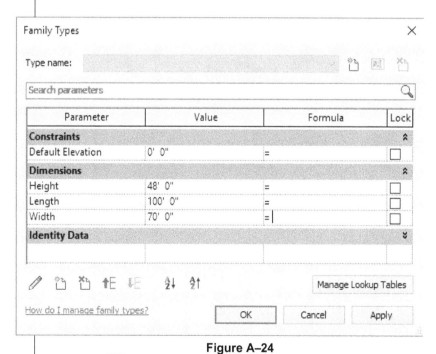

Figure A–24

9. Click (Save).

- In the Family Editor panel, you can click 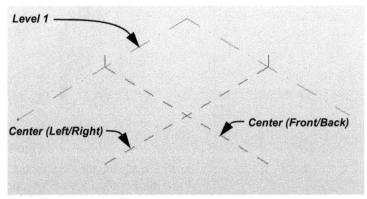 (Load into Project) to load the new mass into an open project.

- Information about creating sketches and forms is covered in the chapter on Massing Studies.

- The Conceptual Mass family template contains one level and two reference planes, as shown in Figure A–25.

You can click on the edge of the levels or reference planes to set the work plane.

Figure A–25

- To select another level by default, open its plan view. Alternatively, select the level marker in a 3D view, as shown in Figure A–26.

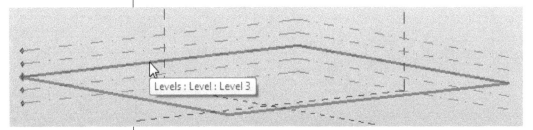

Levels : Level : Level 3

Figure A–26

- The background of 3D views in the Conceptual Mass family file displays as a light gray gradient.

Reference Based Forms

If you want an extruded form or a sweep to retain its shape along the path when the related parameters are flexed, you can make the profile lines a reference. Select the profile lines as though you are going to make a form. Before selecting the Form command, in Properties, in the *Identity Data* category, select **Is Reference Line**.

Before you set the profile as a reference, the lines display, as shown in Figure A–27.

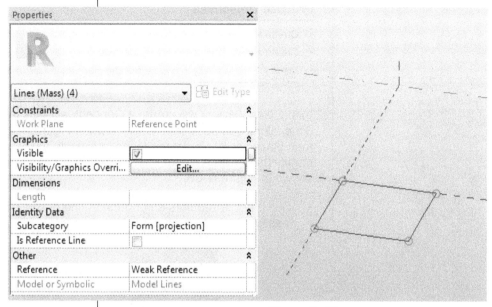

Figure A–27

Once you have set them as a reference, the Properties change and you see reference planes along the edges of the profile, as shown in Figure A–28.

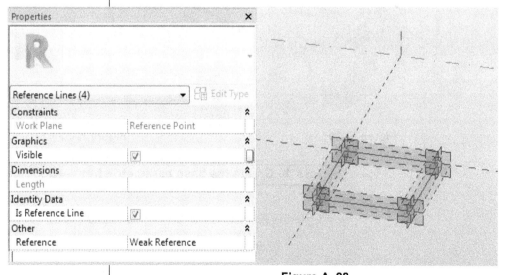

Figure A–28

Practice A2

Advanced Conceptual Massing

Practice Objectives

- Create reference planes and dimension and label them.
- Create a mass form using reference lines.
- Insert the mass family into a project and place instances of it using different parameters.

In this practice, you will create a Conceptual Mass family with dimensions and parameters, as shown in Figure A–29. You will then place two copies of the mass family into a project and modify them using the parameters set up in the mass family, as shown in Figure A–30.

- This practice requires an understanding of conceptual massing and parametric family concepts.

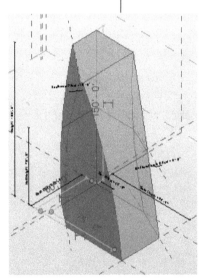

Figure A–29

Figure A–30

Task 1 - Create the base parametric framework.

1. In the *File* tab, expand ☐ (New) and select ☐ (Conceptual Mass).

2. In the New Conceptual Mass - Select Template File dialog box, select the **Mass.rft** template and click **Open**.

3. Save the family as **Edmon-Towers-Model.rfa**.

4. Verify that you are in the **3D Views: {3D}** view and that no other views are open.

5. Open the **Floor Plans: Level 1** view.

6. Enter **WT** to tile the two views and then **ZA** to fit the view in the windows.

7. Working in the 3D view, in the *Create* tab>Draw panel, click

   (Reference Plane).

8. In the Options Bar, set the *Placement Plane* to **Level: Level 1.**

9. Draw the four reference planes shown in Figure A–31. The two angled reference planes should be at different angles.

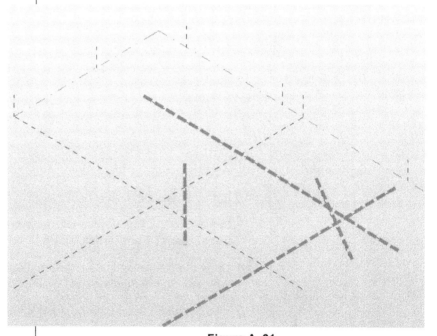

Figure A–31

10. In the plan view, dimension the horizontal and vertical reference planes, label them (instance parameters), and set the values, as shown in Figure A–32.

11. Move the angled lines, if required, to fit inside the footprint of the building. Dimension, but do not label them. Select the reference plane and set the values, as shown in Figure A–32.

Flexing the angles creates additional complexity. Once the rest of the mass works as expected, you can try adding labels and flexing the angles.

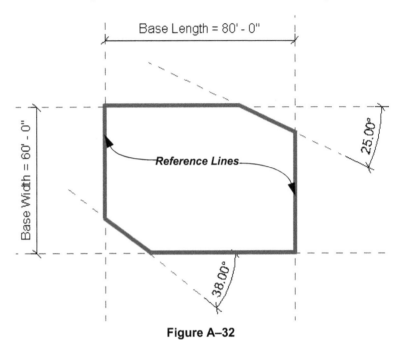

Figure A–32

12. In the *Create* tab>Draw panel, click ↖ (Reference Line).

13. In the Options Bar, verify that *Placement Plane* is still set to **Level: Level 1** and select **Chain**.

14. Draw the reference lines shown in Figure A–32. Ensure that you snap to the intersections of the reference planes.

15. Flex the width and length to ensure that everything works.

16. Save the family.

Task 2 - Create Levels and additional profiles.

Remember that levels in Massing families are not the same as levels in projects. These are for setting heights.

1. Open the **Elevations: South** view.

2. Add two levels, dimension and label them (instance parameters), as shown in Figure A–33. The exact height does not matter at this time.

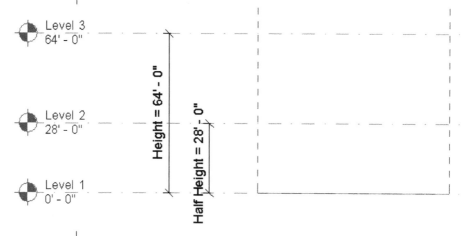

Figure A–33

3. In the *Create* tab>Properties panel, click 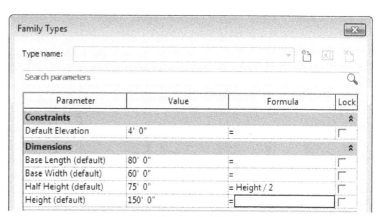 (Family Types).

4. Add a formula to the *Half Height* parameter as shown in Figure A–34. Set the *Height* parameter to **150'-0"** and click **OK**.

Parameter	Value	Formula	Lock
Constraints			⌃
Default Elevation	4' 0"	=	☐
Dimensions			⌃
Base Length (default)	80' 0"	=	☐
Base Width (default)	60' 0"	=	☐
Half Height (default)	75' 0"	= Height / 2	☐
Height (default)	150' 0"	=	☐

Family Types

Type name:

Search parameters

Figure A–34

5. Open the **Floor Plans: Level 2** view.

6. Add two reference planes with labeled dimensions, as shown in Figure A–35.

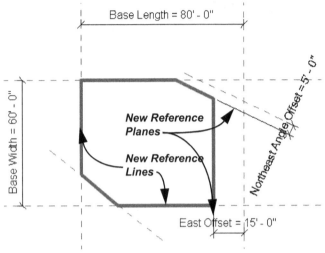

Figure A–35

7. Add Reference Lines on the *Placement Plane:*
   Level: Level 2 using the boundary shown in Figure A–35.

8. Flex the parameters to ensure that they work.

9. Open the **Floor Plans: Level 3** view.

10. Add the Reference Plane, label, and Reference Line boundary, as shown in Figure A–36.

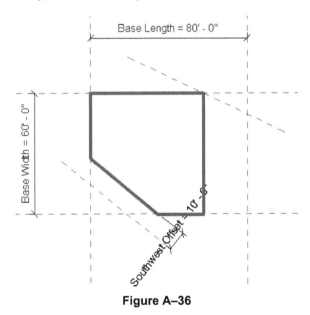

Figure A–36

11. Flex the parameters to test the framework.

12. Save the family.

Task 3 - Create a Mass Form.

1. Open the default 3D view and select the three profiles made of reference lines that should be similar to Figure A–37.

2. In the *Modify | Reference Lines* tab>Form panel, click

    (Create Form). A new mass element should display, as shown in Figure A–38.

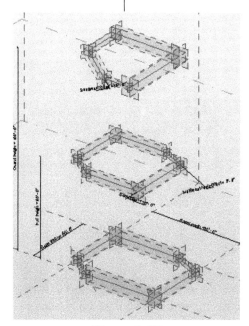

Figure A–37

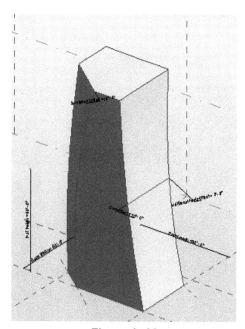

Figure A–38

3. Use the Family Types dialog box to flex the parameters.

4. While in this dialog box, verify that all of the parameters are Instance parameters so they can be modified in a project easily. They should have (default) after the parameter name.

    • If they are not, you can edit them and change them to Instance parameters.

5. In Properties, in the *Other* category, clear the check from **Work Plane-Based**.

6. Save the family.

Task 4 - Use the mass family in a project.

1. Open the project **Edmon-Towers-Study.rvt.**

2. Switch back to the mass family file and load it into the project.

3. Close the alert box.

4. Place two mass families in the new site location, as shown in Figure A–39.

*Mass families can be placed using the **Component** or **Place Mass** commands.*

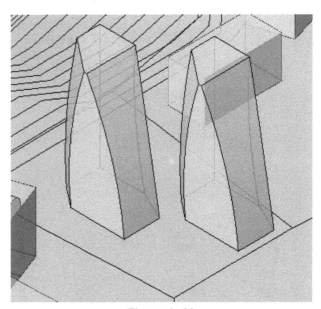

Figure A–39

5. Select one of the mass family elements and in Properties, modify the various dimensions so that the buildings are different.

   • If prompted with a warning suggesting that the type cannot be created, cancel and use a different dimension.

6. Save the project.

Command Summary

Button	Command	Location
Materials		
	Materials	• **Ribbon:** *Manage* tab>Settings panel
	Paint	• **Ribbon:** *Manage* tab>Settings panel
Walkthroughs		
	Edit Walkthrough	• **Ribbon:** *Modify	Cameras* tab> Walkthrough panel
	Export Walkthrough	• **Ribbon:** *File* tab> Export> Images & Animations>Walkthrough
	Open Walkthrough	• **Ribbon:** *Edit Walkthrough* tab> Walkthrough panel
	Walkthrough	• **Ribbon:** *View* tab>Create panel, expand 3D View • **Quick Access Toolbar:** expand 3D View
Conceptual Mass Elements		
	Conceptual Mass	• **Ribbon:** *File* tab>New
	Create Form	• **Family Editor Ribbon:** *Modify	Place Lines* tab> Form panel
	Family Types	• **Family Editor Ribbon:** *Create* or *Modify* tab> Properties panel
	Load into Project	• **Family Editor Ribbon:** All tabs> Family Editor panel
	Load into Project and Close	• **Family Editor Ribbon:** All tabs> Family Editor panel
	Place Mass	• **Ribbon:** *Massing & Site* tab> Conceptual Mass panel

Autodesk Revit Architecture Certification Exam Objectives

The following table will help you to locate the exam objectives in the chapters of the Autodesk® Revit® learning guides to help you prepare for the Autodesk Revit Architecture Certified Professional exam.

Exam Topic	Exam Objective	Learning Guide	Chapter & Section(s)
Collaboration			
	Copy and monitor elements in a linked file	• Revit Collaboration Tools	• 2.3
	Use worksharing	• Revit Collaboration Tools	• 4.1, 4.2, 4.3
	Import DWG and image files	• Revit Fundamentals for Architecture	• 3.4
		• Revit Collaboration Tools	• 3.1, 3.2, 3.3
	Use Worksharing Visualization	• Revit Collaboration Tools	• 4.4
	Assess review warnings in Revit	• Revit Fundamentals for Architecture	• 12.1

Exam Topic	Exam Objective	Learning Guide	Chapter & Section(s)
Documentation			
	Create and modify filled regions	• Revit Fundamentals for Architecture	• 16.3
	Place detail components and repeating details	• Revit Fundamentals for Architecture	• 16.2
	Tag elements (doors, windows, etc.) by category	• Revit Fundamentals for Architecture	• 15.1
	Use dimension strings	• Revit Fundamentals for Architecture	• 14.1
	Set the colors used in a color scheme legend	• Revit Architecture: Conceptual Design and Visualization	• 2.3
	Work with phases	• Revit Collaboration Tools	• 1.1
Elements and Families			
	Change elements within a curtain wall (grids, panels, mullions	• Revit Fundamentals for Architecture	• 6.2, 6.3, 6.4
	Create compound walls	• Revit BIM Management	• 3.1
	Create a stacked wall	• Revit BIM Management	• 3.3
	Differentiate system and component families	• Revit BIM Management	• 3.1 • 4.1
	Work with family parameters	• Revit BIM Management	• 4.2
	Create a new family type	• Revit Fundamentals for Architecture	• 5.3
		• Revit BIM Management	• 4.4
	Use family creation procedures	• Revit BIM Management	• 4.1 to 4.4

Exam Topic	Exam Objective	Learning Guide	Chapter & Section(s)
Modeling			
	Create a building pad	• Revit Architecture: Site and Site Designer	• 1.2
	Define floor for a mass	• Revit Architecture: Conceptual Design and Visualization	• 1.7
	Create a stair with a landing	• Revit Fundamentals for Architecture	• 12.1
	Create elements such as floors, ceilings, or roofs	• Revit Fundamentals for Architecture	• 9.1 • 10.1 • 11.2, 11.4
	Generate a toposurface	• Revit Architecture: Site and Site Designer	• 1.1
	Model railings	• Revit Fundamentals for Architecture	• 12.3
	Edit a model element's material (door, window, furniture)	• Revit Fundamentals for Architecture	• 5.3 • B.4
	Change a generic floor / ceiling / roof to a specific type	• Revit Fundamentals for Architecture	• 9.1 • 10.1 • 11.2
	Attach walls to a roof or ceiling	• Revit Fundamentals for Architecture	• 11.2
	Edit room-aware families	• Revit BIM Management	• 5.1
Views			
	Define element properties in a schedule	• Revit Fundamentals for Architecture	• 15.3
	Control visibility	• Revit Fundamentals for Architecture	• 7.1
	Use levels	• Revit Fundamentals for Architecture	• 3.1
	Create a duplicate view for a plan, section, elevation, drafting view, etc.	• Revit Fundamentals for Architecture	• 7.2
	Create and manage legends	• Revit Fundamentals for Architecture	• 14.4
	Manage view position on sheets	• Revit Fundamentals for Architecture	• 13.2
	Organize and sort items in a schedule	• Revit Fundamentals for Architecture	• B.10
		• Revit BIM Management	• 2.2

Index

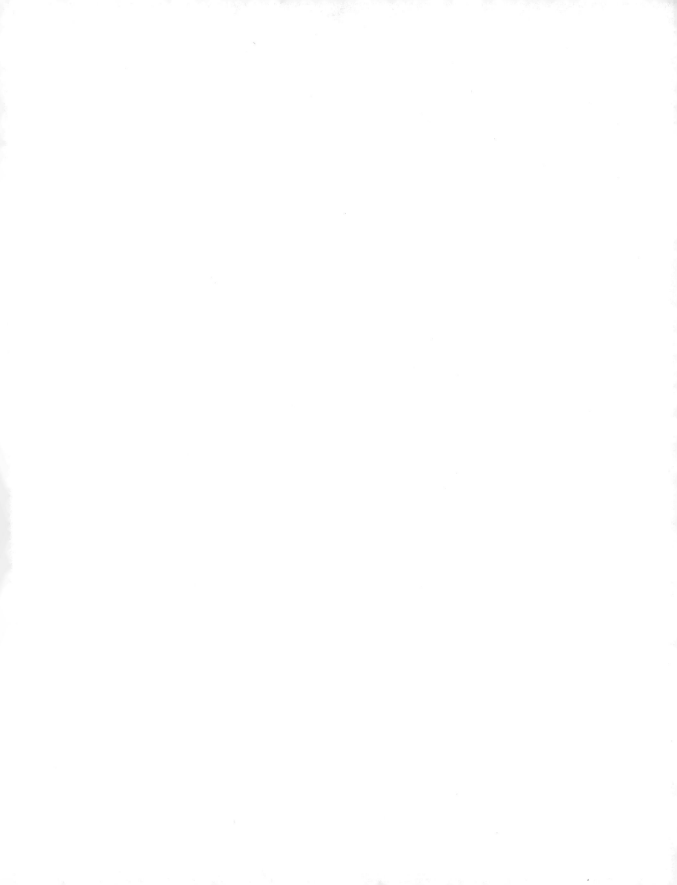

www.ingramcontent.com/pod-product-compliance
Lightning Source LLC
Chambersburg PA
CBHW080404060326
40689CB00019B/4122